D0210167

URBAN
TRAILS
SEATTLE

URBAN TRAILS

TRAILS

SEATTLE

**Shoreline · Renton
Kent · Vashon Island**

CRAIG ROMANO

**MOUNTAINEERS
BOOKS**

MOUNTAINEERS BOOKS is the publishing division of The Mountaineers, an organization founded in 1906 and dedicated to the exploration, preservation, and enjoyment of outdoor and wilderness areas.

1001 SW Klickitat Way, Suite 201, Seattle, WA 98134
800-553-4453, www.mountaineersbooks.org

Copyright © 2018 by Craig Romano
All rights reserved. No part of this book may be reproduced or utilized in any form, or by any electronic, mechanical, or other means, without the prior written permission of the publisher.

Printed in China
Distributed in the United Kingdom by Cordee, www.cordee.co.uk
First edition, 2018

Copyeditor: Rebecca Jaynes
Design: Jen Grable
Layout: Jennifer Shontz, www.redshoedesign.com
Cartographer: Lohnes+Wright
Cover photograph: *A sunny day in Discovery Park (Trail 16)*
    (Photo © Trevor Tinker/Getty Images)
Frontispiece: *Burke-Gilman Trail near Fremont Bridge (Trail 18)*
All photographs by the author unless noted otherwise.

Library of Congress Cataloging-in-Publication Data is on file.

Mountaineers Books titles may be purchased for corporate, educational, or other promotional sales, and our authors are available for a wide range of events. For information on special discounts or booking an author, contact our customer service at 800-553-4453 or mbooks@mountaineersbooks.org.

Printed on FSC®-certified materials

ISBN (paperback): 978-1-68051-032-4
ISBN (ebook): 978-1-68051-033-1

MIX
Papper från
ansvarsfulla källor
FSC® C008047
FSC
www.fsc.org

CONTENTS

SEATTLE

VASHON AND BLAKE ISLANDS

SOUTH KING COUNTY

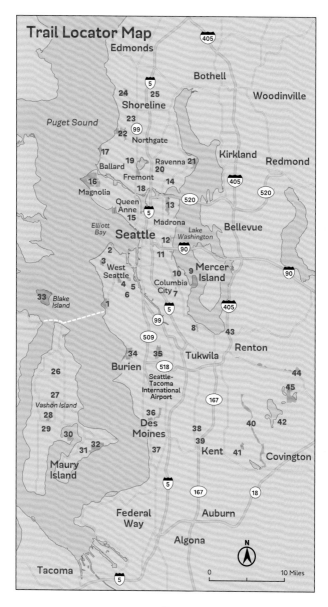

Trail Locator Map

Edmonds

405

Bothell

Woodinville

5

24   25
Shoreline

Puget Sound

23

99

22   Northgate

Kirkland   Redmond

17

19   Ravenna 21
Ballard   20
Fremont   14
16   18
Magnolia   Queen   13   520
Anne   15   Madrona

405

520

5

Elliott
Bay   Seattle   Lake
Washington   Bellevue

2   12
11   90
3
West   10   9   Mercer
Seattle   4   5   Columbia   Island   90
6   City   7

33   Blake
Island   1   5

99   8   43
509   405

34   35   Renton
Burien   Tukwila   44
26   518   45
Seattle-
27   Tacoma
Vashon Island   International
28   Airport   167
29   30   36   40   42
31   32   Des   38
Moines   39
Maury   37   Kent   41   Covington
Island

5

167   18

Federal   Auburn
Way

Algona

N

Tacoma   5   0   10 Miles

TRAILS AT A GLANCE

Trail and/or Park	Distance	Walk	Hike	Run	Kids	Dogs
SEATTLE						
1. Lincoln Park	5 miles of trails	•		•	•	•
2. Alki Trail	5 miles one-way	•		•	•	•
3. Schmitz Preserve Park	1.5 miles of trails	•	•			•
4. Camp Long	3 miles of trails	•	•	•	•	•
5. Duwamish Trail	3.4 miles roundtrip	•		•		
6. Longfellow Creek Legacy Trail	4.2 miles one-way	•		•	•	•
7. Chief Sealth Trail	4.3 miles one-way	•		•	•	•
8. Lakeridge Park	1 mile roundtrip	•	•		•	•
9. Seward Park	4.5 miles of trails	•	•	•	•	•
10. Lake Washington Trail	3.3 miles one-way	•		•	•	•
11. I-90 Trail	5.5 miles roundtrip	•		•	•	•
12. Frink and Leschi Parks	2 miles of trails	•	•	•	•	•
13. Washington Park Arboretum	7 miles of trails	•	•	•	•	•
14. Union Bay Natural Area	1.5 miles of trails	•	•		•	
15. Elliott Bay Trail	5.3 miles one-way	•		•	•	•
16. Discovery Park	more than 12 miles of trails	•	•	•	•	•
17. Golden Gardens Park	more than 3 miles of trails	•	•	•	•	•
18. Burke-Gilman Trail	more than 20 miles one-way	•		•	•	•

Trail and/or Park	Distance	Walk	Hike	Run	Kids	Dogs
19. Green Lake and Woodland Parks	more than 7 miles of trails	•		•	•	•
20. Cowen and Ravenna Parks	more than 4 miles of trails	•	•	•	•	•
21. Warren G. Magnuson Park	more than 4 miles of trails	•	•	•	•	•
22. Carkeek Park	6 miles of trails	•	•	•	•	•
23. Interurban Trail (North)	4.4 miles one-way	•		•	•	•
24. Boeing Creek Park (Shoreline)	3 miles of trails	•	•	•	•	•
25. Hamlin Park (Shoreline)	5 miles of trails	•		•	•	•
VASHON AND BLAKE ISLANDS						
26. Shinglemill Creek Preserve	3 miles roundtrip		•			•
27. Fisher Pond Preserve	3.2 miles of trails		•	•	•	
28. Island Center Forest	more than 10 miles of trails		•	•	•	•
29. Judd Creek Loop Trail	1 mile roundtrip		•		•	•
30. Burton Acres Park	more than 1.5 miles of trails	•	•	•	•	•
31. Dockton Forest and Maury Island Natural Area	more than 10 miles of trails		•	•	•	•
32. Maury Island Marine Park	3 miles of trails	•	•	•	•	•
33. Blake Island Marine State Park	8 miles of trails		•	•	•	•

Trail and/or Park	Distance	Walk	Hike	Run	Kids	Dogs
SOUTH KING COUNTY						
34. Seahurst Park	2.5 miles of trails	•	•	•	•	•
35. North SeaTac Park	more than 5 miles of trails	•		•	•	•
36. Des Moines Creek Trail	4 miles roundtrip	•		•	•	•
37. Saltwater State Park	more than 2 miles of trails	•	•		•	•
38. Interurban Trail (South)	15 miles one-way	•		•	•	•
39. Green River Trail	19.6 miles one-way	•		•	•	•
40. Soos Creek Trail	5.7 miles one-way	•		•	•	•
41. Clark Lake Park	2.5 miles of trails	•		•	•	•
42. Lake Youngs Trail	9.5-mile loop	•		•	•	•
43. Gene Coulon Memorial Beach Park	1.5 miles of trails	•		•	•	
44. Cedar River Trail	17.3 miles one-way	•		•	•	•
45. Spring Lake/ Lake Desire and McGarvey Parks	more than 11 miles of trails		•	•	•	•

Hikers admiring spring blossoms at Washington Park Arboretum (Trail 13)

INTRODUCTION
TRAILS FOR FUN AND FITNESS
IN YOUR BIG BACKYARD

LET'S FACE IT: WHETHER YOU'RE a hiker, walker, or runner, life can get in the way when it comes to putting time in on the trail. Far too often, it's hard for most of us to set aside an hour—never mind a day, or even longer—to hit the trails of our favorite parks and forests strewn across the state. But that doesn't mean we can't get out on the trail more frequently. Right in and near our own communities are thousands of acres of parks and nature preserves containing hundreds of miles of trails. And we can visit these pocket wildernesses, urban and urban-fringe parks and preserves, greenbelts, and trail corridors on a whim, for an hour or two, without having to drive far. Some of these places we can even visit without driving at all—hopping on the bus instead—lessening our carbon footprint while giving ourselves more time to relax.

Urban Trails: Seattle focuses on the myriad trails, parks, and preserves within the urban, suburban, and rural-fringe areas in Seattle, Burien, Des Moines, Kent, Renton, Shoreline, and Vashon and Blake islands. You'll find trails to beaches, old-growth forests, lakeshores, riverfronts, shorelines, wildlife-rich wetlands, rolling hills, scenic vistas, meadows, historic sites, and vibrant neighborhoods and communities. While we often equate hiking trails with the state's wildernesses and forests, there are plenty of areas of natural beauty and accessible trails in the midst of our population centers. The routes included here are designed to show you where you can go for a good run, long walk, or quick hike right in your own backyard.

This guide has two missions. One is to promote fitness and get you outside more often! A trip to Mount Rainier, North Cascades, or Olympic national parks can be a major undertaking. But a quick outdoor getaway to a local park or trail can be done almost anytime—before work, during a lunch break, after work, or when we don't feel like fighting traffic and driving for miles. And all these trails are available year-round, so you can walk, run, or hike every day by utilizing the trails within your own neighborhood. If you feel you are not getting outside enough or getting enough exercise, this book can help you achieve a healthier lifestyle.

Mission number two of this guide is to promote the local parks, preserves, and trails that exist within and near our urban areas. More than 4.7 million people (65 percent of the state's population) call the greater Puget Sound home. While conservationists continue to promote protection of our state's large, roadless wild corners—and that is still important—it's equally important that we promote the preservation of natural areas and develop more trails and greenbelts right where people live. Why? For one thing, the Puget Sound area contains unique and threatened ecosystems that deserve to be protected as much as our wilder remote places. And we need to have usable and accessible trails where people live, work, and spend the majority of their time. Urban trails and parks allow folks to bond with nature and be outside on a regular basis. They help us cut our carbon footprint by giving us access to recreation without burning excessive gallons of fuel to reach a destination. They make it easier for us to commit to regular exercise programs, giving us safe and agreeable places to walk, run, and hike. And urban trails and parks also

Great blue heron at Union Bay Natural Area (Trail 14)

allow for disadvantaged populations—folks who may not have cars or the means to travel to one of our national parks or forests—a chance to experience nature and a healthy lifestyle too. As the greater Puget Sound area continues to grow in population and becomes increasingly more developed, it is all the more important that we support the expansion of our urban parks and trails.

So get out there, get fit, and have fun! And don't forget to advocate for more trails and parks.

Deer are numerous at Lake Youngs (Trail 42).

HOW TO USE
THIS GUIDE

THIS EASY-TO-USE GUIDE PROVIDES YOU with enough details to get out on the trail with confidence while leaving enough room for your own personal discovery. I have walked, hiked, or run every mile of trails described here, and the directions and advice are accurate and up-to-date. Conditions can and do change, however, so make sure you check on the status of a park or trail before you go.

THE DESTINATIONS

This book includes forty-five destinations, covering trails in and around Seattle, Burien, Des Moines, Kent, Renton, Shoreline, and Vashon and Blake islands. Each one begins with the park or trail name followed by a block of information detailing the following:

Distance. Here you will find roundtrip mileage (unless otherwise noted) if the route describes a single trail, or the total mileage of trails within the park/preserve/greenbelt if the route gives an overview of the destination's trail system. Note that while I have measured most of the trails in this book with GPS and have consulted maps and governing land agencies, the distance stated may not always be exact—but it'll be pretty darn close.

Elevation gain. For individual trails, elevation gain is for the *cumulative* difference on the route (and return), meaning not only the difference between the high and low points on the trail, but also for all other significant changes in elevation along the way. For destinations where multiple routes are given, as in a trail network within a park, the elevation gain applies to the steepest trail on the route.

High point. The high point is the highest elevation of the trail or trail system described. Almost all the trails in the book are at a relatively low elevation, ensuring mostly snow-free winter access.

Difficulty. This factor is based not only on length and elevation gain of a trail or trails, but also on the type of tread and surface area of the trail(s). Most of the trails in this book are easy or moderate for the average hiker, walker, or runner. Depending on your level of fitness, you may find the trails more or less difficult than described.

Fitness. This description denotes whether the trail is best for hikers, walkers, or runners. Generally, paved trails will be of more interest to walkers and runners, while rough, hilly trails will appeal more to hikers. Of course you are free to hike, walk, or run (unless running is specifically prohibited) on any of the trails in this book.

Family-friendly. Here you'll find notes on a trail's or park's suitability for children and any cautions to be aware of, such as cliffs, heavy mountain-bike use, and so on. Some trails may be noted as suitable for jogger-strollers and ADA-accessible.

Dog-friendly. This denotes whether dogs are allowed on the trail and what regulations (such as leashed and under control) apply.

Statue of Liberty replica at Alki Beach (Trail 2)

Amenities. The featured park's amenities can include privies, drinking water, benches, interpretive signs/displays, shelters, learning centers, and campgrounds, to name a few.

Contact/map. Here you'll find contact information for getting current trail conditions. All websites and phone numbers for trail and park managers or governing agencies can be found in the Resources section. These websites will often direct you to trail and park maps; in some cases, a better or supplemental map is noted (such as Green Trails).

GPS. GPS coordinates are provided for the main trailhead to help get you to the trail.

Before you go. This section notes any fees or permits required, hours the park or preserve is open (if limited), closures, and any other special concerns.

Next, I describe how to get to the trailhead via your own vehicle or by public transport if available.

GETTING THERE. Driving: Provides directions to the trailhead—generally from the nearest freeway exit, major road, and in the case of Vashon Island, ferry terminal. Often I state directions from more than one destination, and I provide parking information. **Transit:** If the trailhead is served by public transportation, this section identifies the bus agency and line.

EACH HIKE begins with an overview of the featured park or trail, highlighting its setting and character, with notes on the property's conservation history.

GET MOVING. This section describes the route or trails and what you might find on your hike, walk, or run, and may note additional highlights beyond the trail itself, such as points of historical interest.

GO FARTHER. Here you'll find suggestions for making your hike, walk, or run longer within the featured park—or perhaps by combining this trip with an adjacent park or trail.

Artist Jennifer Dixon's FlipBooks along the Interurban Trail (Trail 23)

PERMITS, REGULATIONS, AND PARK FEES

Many of the trails and parks described in this book are managed by county and city parks departments, requiring no permits or fees. Destinations managed by Washington State Parks and the Washington State Department of Natural Resources (DNR) require a day-use fee in the form of the Discover Pass (www.discoverpass.wa.gov) for vehicle access. A Discover Pass can be purchased per vehicle per day or annually for up to two vehicles. You can purchase the pass online, at many retail outlets, or better yet, from a state park office to avoid the handling fee. Each hike in this book clearly states if a fee is charged or a pass is required.

Regulations such as whether dogs are allowed or a park has restricted hours or is closed for certain occasions (such as during high fire danger or for wildlife management) are clearly spelled out in the chapter information blocks.

ROAD AND TRAIL CONDITIONS

In general, trails change little year to year. But change can occur, and sometimes very quickly. A heavy storm can wash out sections of trail or access road in moments. Windstorms can blow down multiple trees across trails, making paths impassable. Lack of adequate funding is also responsible for trail neglect and degradation. For some of the wilder destinations in this book it is wise to contact the appropriate land manager after a significant weather event to check on current trail and road conditions.

On the topic of trail conditions, it is vital that we acknowledge the thousands of volunteers who donate tens of thousands of hours to trail maintenance each year. The Washington Trails Association (WTA) alone coordinates more than 150,000 hours of volunteer trail maintenance each year. But there is always a need for more. Our trail system faces ever-increasing threats, including lack of adequate funding.

Consider joining one or more of the trail and conservation groups listed in the Resources section.

OUTDOOR ETHICS

Strong, positive outdoor ethics include making sure you leave the trail (and park) in as good a condition as you found it—or even better. Get involved with groups and organizations that safeguard, watchdog, and advocate for land protection. And get on the phone and keyboard, and let land managers and public officials know how important protecting lands and trails is to you.

All of us who recreate in Washington's natural areas have a moral obligation and responsibility to respect and protect our natural heritage. Everything we do on the planet has an impact—and we should strive to have as little negative impact as possible. The Leave No Trace Center for Outdoor Ethics is an educational, nonpartisan, nonprofit organization that was developed for responsible enjoyment and active steward-ship of the outdoors. Their program helps educate outdoor enthusiasts about their recreational impacts and recom-mends techniques to prevent and minimize such impacts. While geared toward backcountry use, many Leave No Trace (LNT) principles are also sound advice for urban and urban-fringe parks too, including: plan ahead, dispose of waste properly, and be considerate of other visitors. Visit www.lnt.org to learn more.

TRAIL ETIQUETTE

We need to be sensitive not only to the environment sur-rounding our trails, but to other trail users as well. Some of the trails in this book are also open to mountain bikers and equestrians. When you encounter other trail users, the only hard-and-fast rule is to follow common sense and exercise simple courtesy. With this Golden Rule of Trail Etiquette firmly

Young hiker taking a break at the North Beach (Trail 16)

in mind, here are other things you can do to make everyone's trip more enjoyable:

- **Observe the right-of-way.** When meeting bicyclists or horseback riders, those of us on foot should move off the trail. This is because hikers, walkers, and runners are more mobile and flexible than other users, making it easier for us to quickly step off the trail.

- **Move aside for horses.** When meeting horseback riders, step off the downhill side of the trail unless the terrain makes this difficult or dangerous. In that case, move to the uphill side of the trail, but crouch down a bit so you do not tower over the horses' heads. Also, make yourself visible so as not to spook the big beasties, and talk in a normal voice to the riders. This calms the horses. If walking with a dog, keep your buddy under control.

- **Stay on trails.** Don't cut switchbacks, take shortcuts, or make new trails; all lead to erosion and unsightly trail degradation.

- **Obey the rules specific to the trail or park you are visiting.** Many trails are closed to certain types of use, including dogs and mountain bikes. Some trails are bike only—don't walk on them.

- **Keep dogs under control.** Trail users who bring dogs should have them on a leash or under very strict voice command at all times. And if leashes are required, then this *does* apply to you. Many trail users who have had negative experiences with dogs (actually with the dog owners) on the trail are not fond of, or are even afraid of, encountering dogs. Respect their right *not* to be approached by your darling pooch. A well-behaved leashed dog, however, can certainly help warm up these folks to a canine encounter.

- **Avoid disturbing wildlife.** Observe from a distance, resisting the urge to move closer to wildlife (use your telephoto lens). This not only keeps you safer but also prevents the animal from having to exert itself unnecessarily to flee from you.

- **Take only photographs.** Leave all natural features and historic artifacts as you found them for others to enjoy.

- **Never roll rocks off of trails or cliffs.** Gravity increases the impact of falling rocks exponentially, and you risk endangering lives below you.

Yellow-headed blackbird spotted at Union Bay Natural Area (Trail 14)

- **Mind the music.** Not everyone (almost no one) wants to hear your blaring music. If you like listening to music while you run, hike, or walk, wear headphones and respect other trail users' right to peace and quiet—and to listening to nature's music.

HUNTING

Nearly all the destinations in this book are closed to hunting. However, Vashon Island's Island Center Forest is open to a limited deer hunt in October. If you prefer not to be out on the trail during this short hunting season, check with King County Parks as to the dates, since these change from year to year. While using trails in areas frequented by hunters, it is best to make yourself visible by donning an orange cap and vest. If hiking with a dog, your buddy should wear an orange vest too.

WATER AND GEAR

While most of the trails in this book can be enjoyed without much preparation or gear, it is always a good idea to bring water, even if you're just out for a quick walk or run.

THE TEN ESSENTIALS

If you are heading out for a longer adventure—perhaps an all-day hike in one of Vashon Island's large parks—consider packing **The Ten Essentials**, items that are good to have on hand in an emergency:

1 **Navigation.** Carry a map of the area and know how to read it. A cell phone and GPS unit are good to have along too.

2 **Sun protection.** Even on wet days, carry sunscreen and sunglasses; you never know when the clouds will lift.

3 **Insulation.** Storms can and do blow in rapidly. Carry raingear, wind gear, and extra layers.

4 **Illumination.** If caught out after dark, you'll be glad you have a headlamp or flashlight.

5 **First-aid supplies.** At the very least, your kit should include bandages, gauze, scissors, tape, tweezers, pain relievers, antiseptics, and perhaps a small manual.

6 **Fire.** While being forced to spend the night out is not likely on these trails, a campfire could provide welcome warmth in an emergency, with matches kept dry in a zip-lock bag.

7 **Knife or multitool and repair kit.** A pocketknife or multitool can come in handy, as can basic repair items such as nylon cord, safety pins, a small roll of duct tape, and a small tube of superglue.

8 **Nutrition.** Pack a handful of nuts or sports bars for emergency pick-me-ups.

9 **Hydration.** Bring enough water to keep you hydrated, and for longer treks consider a means of water purification.

10 Emergency shelter. This can be as simple as a garbage bag, or a rain poncho that can double as an emergency tarp.

TRAIL CONCERNS

By and large, our parks and trails are safe places. Common sense and vigilance, however, are still in order. This is true for all trail users, but particularly so for solo ones. Be aware of your surroundings at all times. Let someone know when you're headed out and where you're going.

Sadly, car break-ins are a common occurrence at some of our parks and trailheads. Never leave anything of value in your vehicle while out on the trail. Take your wallet and cell phone with you. A duffel bag on the back seat may contain dirty T-shirts, but a thief may think there's a laptop in it. Save yourself the hassle of returning to a busted window by not giving criminals a reason to clout your car.

A NOTE ABOUT SAFETY

Safety is an important concern in all outdoor activities. No guidebook can alert you to every hazard or anticipate the limitations of every reader. Therefore, the descriptions of roads, trails, routes, and natural features in this book are not representations that a particular place or excursion will be safe for your party. When you follow any of the routes described in this book, you assume responsibility for your own safety. Under normal conditions, such excursions require the usual attention to traffic, road and trail conditions, weather, terrain, the capabilities of your party, and other factors. Because many of the lands in this book are subject to development or change of ownership, conditions may have changed since this book was written that make your use of some of these routes unwise. Always check for current conditions, obey posted private property signs, and avoid confrontations with property owners or managers. Keeping informed on current conditions and exercising common sense are the keys to a safe, enjoyable outing.

—Mountaineers Books

MAP LEGEND

Interstate Highway	Picnic Area
US Highway	Campground/Campsite
State Highway	View/Overlook
Surface Road	Summit
Unpaved Road	Building/Landmark
Hiking Route	River/Stream
Stairs	Lake
Other Trail	Wetland/Marsh
Start	Park/Open Space
Alternative Start	Bridge
Parking	Gate
Restrooms	Tunnel

Vagrants and substance abuse are concerns at some of our urban parks as well. Homelessness is a big issue in Seattle and will continue to be until we address its underlying causes: mental illness, drug and alcohol abuse, and lack of affordable housing. In general, it's best not to wander off trails, and if you come upon a homeless encampment, leave the area and report the situation to the authorities. Be aware of needles, human waste, and other hazardous debris around such encampments. I have omitted parks and trails where this is a serious concern.

There is no need to be paranoid, though—our trails and parks are fairly safe places. Just use a little common sense and vigilance while you're out and about.

Next page: *Along the beach at Lincoln Park (Trail 1)*

SEATTLE

A thriving city of more than 700,000 residents within a metropolitan area of nearly four million, Seattle is one of America's great cities. The eighteenth-largest city in the country within the nation's fifteenth-largest metropolitan area, Seattle is a big city. But there are few large cities in North America that sit in such a stunning natural setting, surrounded by sparkling water (salt and fresh) and two ranges of snowcapped, thickly forested mountains—including one lofty 14,411-foot giant, Mount Rainier.

Thanks to an incredible landscape, the foresight of early city planners to design and build a world-class park system, a city and county government that value trails, and an active population engaged in a healthy outdoor lifestyle, when it comes to urban trails, Seattle is top-notch. The city's large park system contains a wide array of trails that traverse manicured lawns, nature preserves, old-growth forest groves, historic districts, and vibrant neighborhoods—as well as trails that travel along lakeshores, cascading creeks, and stretches of Puget Sound shoreline.

Within this sprawling metropolis you'll also find some of the best long-distance paved trails in the Northwest. They thread together parks and greenbelts that call out for further exploration and adventures. Hike, run, or walk Seattle's urban trails. There are hundreds of miles of them, giving you many reasons to never leave the city when seeking excellent outdoor adventures.

1   Lincoln Park

DISTANCE:	About 5 miles of trails
ELEVATION GAIN:	Up to 200 feet
HIGH POINT:	160 feet
DIFFICULTY:	Easy to moderate
FITNESS:	Walkers, runners
FAMILY-FRIENDLY:	Yes, and some trails are jogger-stroller and wheelchair accessible
DOG-FRIENDLY:	On leash
AMENITIES:	Restrooms, picnic tables, interpretive signs, benches, water, playground, playfield, pool
CONTACT/MAP:	Seattle Parks and Recreation
GPS:	N47 31.613 W122 23.579
BEFORE YOU GO:	Park is open from 4:00 AM to 11:30 PM

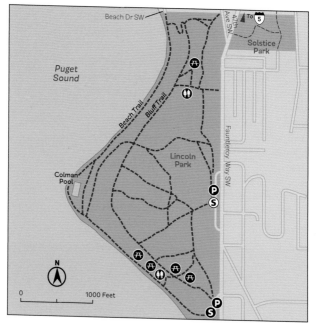

GETTING THERE

Driving: From downtown Seattle, follow I-5 south to exit 163A (from South Seattle, follow I-5 north to exit 163). Then continue west on Spokane Street Viaduct to West Seattle Bridge for 2.8 miles to Fauntleroy Way SW. Continue on Fauntleroy Way SW for 2.7 miles to parking and trailheads (more parking is available 0.3 mile south).

Transit: King County Metro routes RapidRide C, 116, 118, and 119

One of the best places in Seattle for a shoreline sunset stroll, Lincoln Park's 1-mile trail along seawall and rocky beach is hard to beat. Its 1-mile bluff-top trail is spectacular too, offering sublime views of the Olympic Mountains across the Sound framed by overhanging old-growth greenery. Watch ferries plying the Sound, squirrels scurrying up big trees, and waves lapping away your worries.

GET MOVING

Much of West Seattle's Lincoln Park is adorned with towering old-growth maples, madronas, cedars, and Douglas firs. But it's the park's Puget Sound frontage that the majority of visitors cherish most. Walk this path—paved at first and then gravel north of the pool—anytime of the day, anytime of the year to relish the ever-changing beauty and moods of the Salish Sea. Storms bring crashing waves. Sunsets bring shimmering waters and sensational seascapes.

You can make a 2-mile loop by walking the beach trail to a connector trail that takes off uphill, just before Beach Drive SW. This path tackles the high shoreline bluff via steps and tight switchbacks, definitely raising your pulse. Then walk back on the pleasant Bluff Trail, which is level at first, then gently slopes downward. There are forest-framed sound views along the way and some impressive trees. About midway you can head back to the beach on a well-graded trail. In the summer,

Lincoln Park's Beach Trail at sunset

consider a post-workout splash in the heated saltwater Colman Pool.

The park's upland is traversed by many interconnecting trails, some leading to busy playfields, playgrounds, and picnic grounds, and others to quiet and peaceful forest groves.

GO FARTHER

Carefully cross Fauntleroy Way SW near the park's northeast corner and check out Solstice Park. Walk a short trail, complete with steps, up an artificial hill (built to stabilize a slope) to a large astrolabe (here, a big earthen sundial) used to make astronomical measurements. Enjoy some good views of the Sound and Olympic Mountains, and do check out the astrolabe during various lunar and solar events—like a solstice!

2 | **Alki Trail**

DISTANCE:	5 miles one-way
ELEVATION GAIN:	Minimal
HIGH POINT:	30 feet
DIFFICULTY:	Easy
FITNESS:	Walkers, runners
FAMILY-FRIENDLY:	Yes, and jogger-stroller and wheelchair accessible
DOG-FRIENDLY:	On leash
AMENITIES:	Restrooms, bathhouse, picnic tables, interpretive signs, benches, water
CONTACT/MAP:	Seattle Parks and Recreation; Seattle Department of Transportation
GPS:	N47 34.660 W122 24.953
BEFORE YOU GO:	Jack Block Park is open from 6:00 AM to 9:00 PM

GETTING THERE

Driving: From downtown Seattle, follow I-5 south to exit 163A (from South Seattle, follow I-5 north to exit 163). Then continue west on Spokane Street Viaduct to West Seattle Bridge

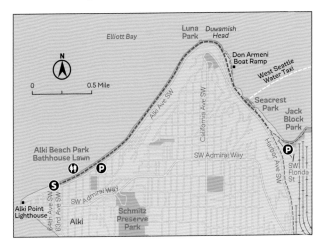

Seattle skyline across Elliott Bay from the Alki Trail

for 2.4 miles and take the Harbor Avenue exit. Proceed west for 0.1 mile on SW Spokane Street and turn right onto Harbor Avenue SW. Now drive north on Harbor Avenue SW, passing street parking for the trail along the way. At 1 mile, come to SW Florida Street on your right, which provides access in

0.2 mile to Jack Block Park. At 1.8 miles, Harbor Avenue SW becomes Alki Avenue SW. You can continue on this road for 1.8 miles to Alki Beach Park. There is limited street parking all along the trail and plentiful parking at Jack Block Park.

Transit: King County Metro routes 37 (limited service), 50, 56 (limited service), DART 773, and DART 775; King County Water Taxi from downtown to West Seattle

Walk along a sprawling shoreline granting stunning views of snowy mountains, sparkling sound, and shiny city skyline. Alki Beach is the birthplace of Seattle. And while much has changed here since 1851 when the first Euro-Americans settled this point, Alki still feels far removed from the city it spawned. Walk past historic monuments and relics, rows of old bungalows, and piers for peering out at some of the finest maritime views in the city. One of the best places in Seattle for people watching too, Alki has a vibrant, diverse, and distinct pulse that feels a little like a cross between the California seaside and an East Coast beach town.

GET MOVING

The paved Alki Trail extends for 5 miles from West Seattle's Alki Beach to East Marginal Way S. in the heart of the city's industrial Duwamish River "delta," but the easternmost 1.5 miles are along busy roads and across Harbor Island; that final segment is best left for commuting bicyclists. The western 3.5 miles, however, is one of the most delightful (and virtually flat) walking and running routes in the city. Legions of locals walk and run this trail almost daily. And an adjacent bike lane along this stretch keeps it pedestrian-only. On your first visit, expect to be distracted by the sights and tempting eateries. Give in to curiosity. Eventually you'll be able to return for a long walk or brisk run with just the lapping waves, cruising watercraft, and lofty peaks and shimmering skyscrapers vying for your attention.

THE FIRST DENNYS IN SEATTLE

While it wasn't until the 1960s that the first Denny's restaurant landed in Seattle, the first Dennys—as in the Denny Party—landed in the area in the 1850s! A group of pioneers led by Arthur A. Denny and including many of his family members left Illinois in the spring of 1851. By wagon and via the Oregon Trail they arrived in Portland in the Oregon Territory in August. Ironically, they found the Willamette Valley crowded and began looking for locations to the north to homestead. David Denny and John Low began scouting sites on Puget Sound and met Lee Terry in the process. Low and Terry staked claims at Alki Beach, not too far from the mouth of the Duwamish River. Low went back to Portland to urge Arthur and others in the group to come to Alki.

On November 13, 1851, the Denny Party, consisting of Arthur Denny, John Low, eight other adults, and twelve children, arrived by schooner at Alki Point. They stayed there in a cabin for the winter—and then all but a few of them set out in the spring looking for a better location. They eventually settled on an island surrounded by mudflats near Elliott Bay (near what is now Pioneer Square in downtown Seattle). They named their settlement Duwamps. Lee Terry's brother Charles stayed in Alki and dubbed his claim New York and later New York Alki. For the next three years the two settlements competed as rival town sites. That spring Doc Maynard joined Arthur Denny and others at the Elliott Bay settlement. Maynard would be responsible for naming the fledgling community Seattle.

Walk the Alki and Elliott Bay trails and look for places named after members of the Denny Party—Denny, Low, Boren, Bell, and Terry. And yes there's a Denny's downtown too. But the city's most famous Denny's—the one in Ballard—despite its architectural and historical significance, is now like the original Alki settlement, no longer to be found.

The trail officially starts near the corner of 64th Avenue SW and Alki Avenue SW. Here too is the beginning of the Mountains to Sound Greenway (http://mtsgreenway.org), an urban and wild corridor that weaves together nearly one million public acres of land along I-90 from Seattle to Ellensburg. The trail traverses Alki Beach Park, one of the liveliest spots (especially on a warm summer day) in the city. Enjoy breathtaking views of the Olympic Mountains and West Point across Elliott Bay. On clear days, Mount Baker can be seen behind Queen Anne Hill. The Space Needle is clearly visible too—but not (yet) the downtown towers.

Continue through the park, walking northeast along one of the city's most scenic shorelines. Pass or pause at interpretive signs, historical sites, and eclectic landmarks, including a stone from Plymouth Rock in Massachusetts and a miniature Statue of Liberty. You'll also pass a plaque commemorating the Denny Party (see sidebar "The first Dennys in Seattle"), which settled here in 1851, beginning the transformation of this wild corner of Native land into one of the country's major metropolitan areas.

Now pass a fine sandy beach and beach volleyball courts that bustle in summer. The entire area takes on the air of a resort in the warmer months. Alki was once a destination spot, lined with cottages and serviced by a trolley from "the city." Several of the old bungalows still stand, shadowed by new skinny high-rises and large modern homes.

At 1.8 miles, round Duwamish Head, hemmed in by a treed bluff to the south. Here Elliott Bay and the Seattle skyline in its entirety are revealed. So too is Mount Rainier, floating above the loading docks on Harbor Island. This is a great spot to watch the flotilla of vessels—from tugs to barges to ferries—ply the bay. From 1907 to 1913, this spot was the site of Luna Park, an extravagant amusement park complete with a roller coaster.

The trail now narrows and continues southeast, passing piers, a boat ramp, and a popular diving area. At 2.4 miles reach Seacrest Park. Here the West Seattle Water Taxi (www .kingcounty.gov/transportation) operates a route to Pier 50 downtown. The trail continues, passing waterfront restaurants and a piece of the historic MV *Kalakala* ferry. At 3 miles come to the entrance of Jack Block Park. This 15-acre park, owned by the Port of Seattle, contains manicured walking paths, a long pier, a children's play area, a small beach, and a 45-foot-high observation tower offering sweeping city views. It's a great spot to spend some time and the perfect spot for turning around. Beyond this park, the Alki Trail leaves the shoreline to parallel Harbor Avenue SW for 0.8 mile before utilizing sidewalks and busy bike lanes on its way to Harbor Island and the Elliott Bay Trail near East Marginal Way S.

GO FARTHER

Combine this trail with the Elliott Bay Trail (Trail 15) for a grand walk or run around Seattle's busy waterfront. You can skip (recommended) the industrial and unattractive parts of both of these trails by hopping on the water taxi. You can also easily add a trip to Schmitz Preserve Park (Trail 3) by walking two blocks south on 58th Avenue SW to the trailhead.

3 Schmitz Preserve Park

DISTANCE:	1.5 miles of trails
ELEVATION GAIN:	Up to 275 feet
HIGH POINT:	300 feet
DIFFICULTY:	Easy to moderate
FITNESS:	Walkers, hikers
FAMILY-FRIENDLY:	Yes
DOG-FRIENDLY:	On leash
AMENITIES:	None, but restrooms and water can be found at the adjacent Alki Playground and Whale Tail Park
CONTACT/MAP:	Seattle Parks and Recreation
GPS:	N47 34.653 W122 24.390
BEFORE YOU GO:	Park is open from 6:00 AM to 10:00 PM

GETTING THERE

Driving: From downtown Seattle, follow I-5 south to exit 163A (from South Seattle, follow I-5 north to exit 163). Then continue

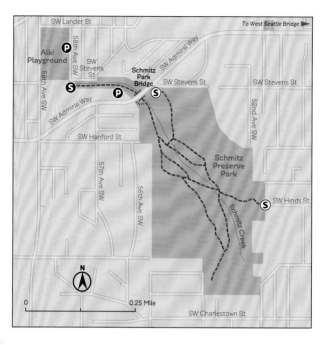

west on Spokane Street Viaduct to West Seattle Bridge for 2.4 miles and take the Admiral Way exit. Follow SW Admiral Way for 2.5 miles, then turn right onto 59th Avenue SW. Drive one block north to Alki Playground. Park on the street and find the trailhead (old gated road) on the east side of Alki Elementary.

Transit: King County Metro routes 50, 56 (limited service), 57 (limited service), and DART 775

Wander through a ravine harboring a piece of a Seattle long gone—a tract of ancient forest. Just blocks from bustling Alki Beach, Schmitz Preserve Park contains towering firs, cedars, and hemlocks hundreds of years old. Walk within this primeval patch of emerald glory and quickly lose the hum of vehicles to the lull of a babbling creek and the melodious songs of wrens and thrushes. You'll soon forget you're in a city of 700,000 people.

GET MOVING

Schmitz Preserve Park consists of 53 acres of thick forest tucked within a deep ravine surrounded by city blocks. The park was donated to the city in the early part of the 20th century by Ferdinand Schmitz. An immigrant from Germany, Schmitz did quite well for himself as a banker and real estate investor. He served on Seattle's parks commission and saw value in the city retaining a part of its original forest cover. While the park contains old growth and a few big trees, there was some logging in the ravine prior to its establishment as a park. A storm in 1992 claimed quite a few big trees as well. Still, along with Seward Park, this is Seattle's finest ancient forest.

The park is small and contains a network of short intercon-necting trails totaling a little more than 1.5 miles. It's a place to stop and observe rather than tune out and rush forward. Walk the trails with no sense of purpose and you can easily spend a couple of hours here, oblivious to the outside world.

The best way to hike the park is from Alki Playground (also known as Whale Tail Park). Follow a gated old road, signed for Schmitz Park, alongside a creek and up and into a ravine. The old road darts under the Schmitz Park Bridge (SW Admiral Way) and enters the forest primeval. A short trail leads left, crossing the small creek and reaching another old road—which was used until 2002 as the entrance to the park. You can follow this old road left to SW Admiral Way and then cross the bridge and return to the ravine via a stairway on the bridge's north side.

Your other options include two loops, one short and a lon-ger one that traverses steep slopes and offers views down to the ravine floor. Both loops cross the creek, and the longer one travels over a small wetland area via boardwalks. Two other trails radiate from the outer loop. One heads south and

Creek crossing in Schmitz Park's old-growth forest

climbs steeply. It soon peters out beneath a series of windfalls. The other trail heads east and climbs steeply out of the ravine leading to SW Hinds Street—an alternative starting area. For a good workout, hike up and down the radiating trails. And if you want increased mileage, walk the loops in varying order or consider heading over to the Alki Trail (Trail 2) afterward. You can reach it by walking one block north from the Alki Playground.

4 Camp Long

DISTANCE:	3 miles of trails
ELEVATION GAIN:	Up to 200 feet
HIGH POINT:	325 feet
DIFFICULTY:	Easy to moderate
FITNESS:	Walkers, hikers, runners
FAMILY-FRIENDLY:	Yes, and access road/trail is jogger-stroller friendly
DOG-FRIENDLY:	On leash
AMENITIES:	Restrooms, water, climbing wall, cabins, picnic shelters, Environmental Learning Center
CONTACT/MAP:	Seattle Parks and Recreation
GPS:	N47 33.326 W122 22.502
BEFORE YOU GO:	Park is open Tuesday–Sunday from 10:00 AM to 6:00 PM (March–October); Tuesday–Saturday from 10:00 AM to 6:00 PM (November–February)

GETTING THERE

Driving: From downtown Seattle, follow I-5 south to exit 163A (from South Seattle, follow I-5 north to exit 163). Then continue west on Spokane Street Viaduct to West Seattle Bridge for 2.7 miles. When you come to a traffic light, turn left onto 35th Avenue SW and drive 0.6 mile south. Then turn left onto SW Dawson Street and continue a couple hundred feet to Camp Long and trailhead parking.

Transit: King County Metro Route 21

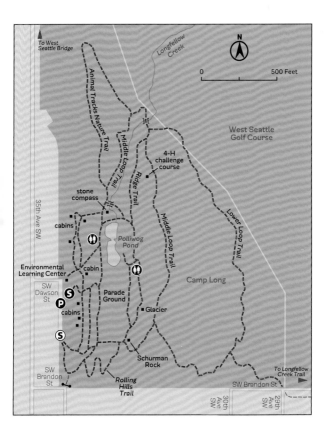

A former Boy Scout camp built by the Depression-era Works Progress Administration (WPA), Camp Long offers deep-in-the-woods ambience right in the city. Graced with rustic cabins (available for rent), a climbing wall, and a 4-H challenge course (not open to the public), the camp sees a steady stream of school and outdoor groups. A few miles of well-groomed trails weave through the property. Follow them to enjoy plenty of natural beauty in one of Seattle's most unique parks.

Stone steps beside Camp Long's "Glacier"

GET MOVING

Originally slated to be part of the West Seattle Golf Course, this 68-acre wooded and wetland tract became a special retreat to teach Scouts outdoor skills, thanks to Judge William Long, mountaineer and Scout leader Clark Schurman, and a couple of other visionaries. In 1984, Camp Long was opened to the general public. The park's rustic and elegant stone lodge has since been transformed into a visitors center and Environmental Learning Center.

There's usually something going on at Camp Long, so be mindful of campers and group activities. But feel free to roam the park, checking out both its natural and human-built features. From the lodge, pass a structure that's sure to have millennials scratching their heads—yes, that's a phone booth! Now either walk down a set of steps or adjacent ramps or take the winding and pleasant Rolling Hills Trail (open to wheel-chairs and jogger-strollers) to the Parade Ground.

Following a closed-to-vehicles gravel service road, march around the Parade Ground. Cabins and picnic shelters face it from the wooded flanks, and Polliwog (tadpole) Pond graces its northern reaches. Walk around the pond on paths, stone steps, and pretty little stone bridges. Near the Parade Ground, check out Schurman Rock, a 20-foot-high climbing rock. You can practice on it, but be sure to keep children well super-vised. The rock was the brainchild of the aforementioned Clark Schurman, an experienced mountaineer who served as the chief guide at Mount Rainier National Park from 1939 to 1942. Camp Schurman on Rainier's north face is also named for him.

To the north of Schurman Rock is another interesting climbing feature, the Glacier. Meant to replicate this landform without ice, this unique rocky structure will also intrigue bud-ding climbers. At the Parade Ground's far north is a beauti-ful stone compass. Here several trails take off. The 0.3-mile Animal Tracks Nature Trail when combined with a portion of the Middle Loop Trail makes a 0.5-mile loop. The Middle Loop Trail combined with the Parade Ground road is just shy of a half mile, and the Lower Loop Trail combined with the Parade Ground road is just over a half mile.

There are a couple of shorter connecter trails between the loops, making it possible to do figure eights. The trails are fairly well built, with a few dips and climbs and a couple of steps here and there. Two of the connectors lead over bridges of a tributary of Longfellow Creek, which flows through a small ravine. While the whole area feels like you're miles from the city, urban noises will constantly be audible. And in winter when leaf cover is sparse, you can often see the Seattle skyline in the distance.

In a cedar grove on the Lower Loop, a short trail heads east and downhill. It leads 0.1 mile to a wetland and park entrance on SW Brandon Street. From here it's possible to cross the road and follow a trail 0.2 mile to the Longfellow Creek Legacy Trail (Trail 6). You can then extend your run/walk/hike following this wonderful urban trail.

5   Duwamish Trail

DISTANCE:	3.4 miles roundtrip
ELEVATION GAIN:	20 feet
HIGH POINT:	30 feet
DIFFICULTY:	Easy
FITNESS:	Walkers, runners
FAMILY-FRIENDLY:	Travels along and through heavily trafficked areas; some questionable activities take place in Herring's House Park
DOG-FRIENDLY:	On leash
AMENITIES:	Restrooms, picnic tables, interpretive signs at Terminal 107 Park
CONTACT/MAP:	King County Parks
GPS:	N47 33.657 W122 21.091
BEFORE YOU GO:	There is a four-hour parking limit at Herring's House Park

GETTING THERE

Driving: From downtown Seattle, follow I-5 south to exit 163A (from South Seattle, follow I-5 north to exit 163). Then continue west on Spokane Street Viaduct for 0.9 mile, taking the Harbor Island exit. Continue straight on Spokane Street

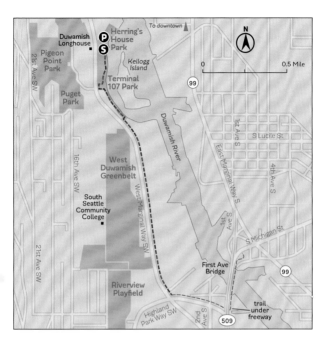

(going over Spokane Street Bridge) for 0.7 mile, bearing right onto West Marginal Way SW. Then continue 0.8 mile to trailhead parking on your left at Herring's House Park.

Transit: King County Metro routes 120, 125, and 131 service Highland Park Way SW

Run or walk along the Duwamish River in the heart of the city's industrial district. Once one of the most productive waterways within Puget Sound, the Duwamish has been channeled and polluted and its extensive, rich estuarine mudflats filled in and paved over. But thanks to conservationists, concerned citizens, tribal members, and enlightened officials, the river is slowly being cleaned up. Follow a paved level path through a couple of pocket parks rife with history and remnants of the past. Walk past a few remaining natural areas where wildlife still makes its home among cargo containers, factories, terminals, and concrete plants.

GET MOVING

Start your Duwamish River (called the Duwamish Waterway where it runs through the city) rambling at Herring's House Park. For centuries this site was home to a Duwamish People's village. But by the late 1800s it was sprouting shanties in the new city of Seattle. A sawmill and a brick factory soon followed. In the 1980s it became a park.

Walk on some of the soft-surface paths traversing this 17-acre park for views of the small tidal flats along the river. The paved Duwamish Trail leaves from the south end of the park (a small section continues north, soon leading to sidewalk). Head upriver to the well-maintained and manicured Port of Seattle's Terminal 107 Park. Divert from the trail to check out some of the paths leading to historic sites, interpretive displays, and a sculpture of a scaled-down skeleton of a North Pacific halibut schooner.

Across busy West Marginal Way from the park is the Duwamish Longhouse and Cultural Center. The center is open to the public, so consider visiting it after your workout. Chief Seattle, whom Doc Maynard named the city of Seattle after, was of Suquamish and Duwamish heritage. The Duwamish Tribe, however, is still not recognized by the federal government.

The trail soon makes a sharp turn left to a bluff, where Puget Creek enters the Duwamish River. Here you can get a good view of Kellogg Island. Unlike Harbor Island at the river's mouth, Kellogg is natural. However, half of the island was destroyed to widen the waterway channel on its east side. Its west side is graced by the last remaining natural curve in the lower waterway. The river and its tributaries have been greatly altered by humans since the early 20th century (see sidebar

Kellogg Island offers a touch of wild in the industrial Duwamish River.

"A River Once Ran Through Here" in Trail 38). Industrialization has taken its toll, and the entire lower waterway has been declared a Superfund site by the EPA. But here at this bend around Kellogg Island, eagles, ospreys, sundry waterfowl, and scores of other critters thrive.

The trail continues south along the river, bending right at a large cement factory. It then crosses some railroad tracks and continues south, paralleling West Marginal Way. On your left is the developed waterway. On your right across the road is the West Duwamish Greenbelt—the largest greenbelt within the city (see "Go Farther"). At 1.7 miles the way bends left to parallel Highland Park Way SW. This is a good turning-around spot for pedestrians. The trail (more a sidewalk) continues 0.8 mile, ducking under SR 509 before reaching S. Michigan Street. Here the route follows busy city streets through South Park before resuming course as a paved trail once again—now as the Green River Trail (Trail 39).

GO FARTHER

While venturing beyond the Highland Park Way junction is not an appealing walk or run, you may want to head the short distance to the pedestrian ramp granting access to the First Avenue Bridge. Walk onto the bridge and enjoy good views of the Duwamish Waterway and feel the industrial pulse of the city.

Nearby and above the waterway are a series of parks and protected lands forming the West Duwamish Greenbelt. You can find several trails of varying conditions here at Pigeon Point Park off of 21st Avenue SW, Puget Park off of SW Dawson Street, Riverview Playfield off of Highland Park Way SW, and Westcrest Park off of 8th Avenue SW. The latter is the most developed of the parks and contains the largest complex of trails. And with a large off-leash area, it is extremely popular with dog-walkers. The park also provides excellent views of the city skyline.

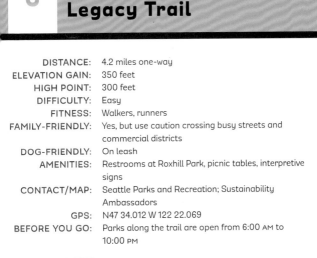

6

Longfellow Creek Legacy Trail

DISTANCE:	4.2 miles one-way
ELEVATION GAIN:	350 feet
HIGH POINT:	300 feet
DIFFICULTY:	Easy
FITNESS:	Walkers, runners
FAMILY-FRIENDLY:	Yes, but use caution crossing busy streets and commercial districts
DOG-FRIENDLY:	On leash
AMENITIES:	Restrooms at Roxhill Park, picnic tables, interpretive signs
CONTACT/MAP:	Seattle Parks and Recreation; Sustainability Ambassadors
GPS:	N47 34.012 W 122 22.069
BEFORE YOU GO:	Parks along the trail are open from 6:00 AM to 10:00 PM

GETTING THERE

Driving to Southern Trailhead: From downtown Seattle, follow I-5 south to exit 163A (from South Seattle, follow I-5 north to exit 163). Then continue west on Spokane Street Viaduct for 1.5 miles, taking the Delridge Way exit. Continue south on Delridge Way SW for 3.4 miles. Then turn right onto SW Barton Place (which becomes SW Barton Street) and drive 0.5 mile. Turn left onto 29th Avenue SW and drive one block to trailhead parking at Roxhill Park. **Driving to Northern Trailhead:** Follow the preceding directions. From the Delridge Way exit, continue on Delridge Way SW for 0.3 mile and turn right onto SW Andover Street. Drive 0.2 mile west and turn left onto 28th Avenue SW. Proceed for one block to the trailhead on your left. Park on the street.

Transit: King County Metro routes 50, 120, and 128 service Delridge Way. RapidRide C, 21, 22, 60, 120, 125, and Sound Transit 560 all service Westwood Village.

Walk or run this undulating 4.2-mile trail that weaves through the Delridge valley between shopping centers and forested greenbelts sliced by a revived creek. Life has returned to this once neglected waterway, one of four urban creeks restored through daylighting and native plantings in the late 1990s by Seattle Public Utilities. Walk through tracts of towering conifers and cottonwoods, a peat bog, and wetland pools. And watch for eagles, kingfishers, salmon, and even beavers.

GET MOVING

Do this trail as an out and back from either direction, or hop on a bus and do it one-way. If one-way is your preference, start from the south to take advantage of the elevation drop and to finish at the trail's highlights: *Dragonfly Pavilion* and *Salmon Bone Bridge*, two public artworks. The description that follows is for south to north.

The trail starts in Roxhill Park, home of a small peat bog representative of what much of this area looked like before urbanization. Longfellow Creek begins here. Find the trail and start your downstream journey. The trail is well-marked with brown posts that denote mileage to parks and features along the way. There are a couple of spots, however, where it is easy to go off course—hopefully this book will keep you literally on the right track.

Cross busy SW Barton Street and begin winding through the Westwood Village shopping center (a good spot to get lunch or coffee). The creek is flowing through pipes below as you negotiate the walkways through the shopping center. Be sure to go right at Bed Bath and Beyond, or you'll end up going beyond the trail. Look for posts and high metal banner signs with dragonflies and other wetland critters to help guide you.

Cross SW Trenton Street and head up a flight of stairs. Then walk through the Southwest Athletic Complex and cross SW Thistle Street. Turn right in front of Chief Sealth High

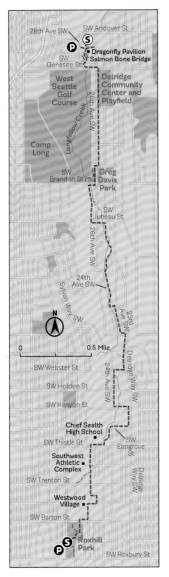

School and pick up bona fide trail again at a community garden. Now enjoy a wonderful stretch of wooded trail—and the creek flowing at your side.

The way then turns right to follow SW Elmgrove Street, left to follow Delridge Way SW (on good sidewalk), and left onto SW Kenyon Street. Pick up trail again, crossing the creek on a bridge, then turn right and walk along 24th Avenue SW. Cross SW Holden Street and pass a detention pond. Then take a right at Home Depot onto SW Webster Street and then a quick left onto Delridge Way SW.

Walk along this busy road for a short way, then turn left onto SW Myrtle Street, right onto 23rd Avenue SW, then left for a bridged crossing of the creek. Next, it's right on quiet 24th Avenue SW before coming to trail. Now enjoy some of the best parts of this walk—through attractive forest and past an artificial beaver dam that harbors waterfowl.

Artist Lorna Jordan's Salmon Bone Bridge

Continue on real trail (occasionally following roadways), crossing the creek a couple of times and weaving through riparian forest. At 3 miles come to a junction in a beautiful cedar grove. Turn right here (the trail left is worth checking out too—and it returns to Longfellow Creek Legacy Trail) and cross the creek. Then cross SW Brandon Street and enter the lovely Greg Davis Park. Feel free to divert on its half mile or so of side trails. You can also walk a short distance west on a trail leading to Camp Long (Trail 4).

The Longfellow Creek Legacy Trail now follows sidewalk on 26th Avenue SW for some distance. At SW Genesee Street, just past the Delridge Community Center and Playfield, make a left. Then soon pick up trail once again and follow the creek through a forested glade. Pass under SW Nevada Street, then cross the creek on the architecturally pleasing *Salmon Bone Bridge*. The trail then comes to a junction. Right leads to SW Dakota Street. You want to go left, winding up an open slope to the beautiful *Dragonfly Garden and Pavilion* and trail's end on 28th Avenue SW.

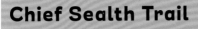

7 Chief Sealth Trail

DISTANCE:	4.3 miles one-way
ELEVATION GAIN:	Up to 800 feet
HIGH POINT:	330 feet
DIFFICULTY:	Easy to moderate
FITNESS:	Walkers, runners
FAMILY-FRIENDLY:	Yes, and paved trail is jogger-stroller friendly
DOG-FRIENDLY:	On leash
AMENITIES:	None
CONTACT/MAP:	Seattle Department of Transportation
GPS:	N47 33.628 W122 18.747
BEFORE YOU GO:	This trail lacks amenities and parking areas along its course. Park on the street or consider parking in spaces along 16th Avenue S. abutting nearby Jefferson Park (restrooms available) and walking 0.25 mile on sidewalks to the northern trailhead on S. Angeline Street.

GETTING THERE

Driving: From downtown Seattle, follow I-5 south to exit 163A (from South King County, follow I-5 north to exit 163). Then continue east on S. Columbian Way for 0.5 mile, merging onto 15th Avenue S. Follow 15th Avenue S. for 0.6 mile and turn left onto S. Angeline Street. Drive 300 feet to the trailhead on your right and park on street.

Transit: King County Metro routes 36, 50 (near north trailhead), 106, and 107 (near south trailhead); trail is also accessible via Sound Transit Link light rail, Rainier Beach Station

You'll get a good workout indeed if you run or walk the Chief Sealth Trail from end to end—and back! This paved path sets out on a rolling course, following a green swath beneath a pair of powerlines. There are a few good grades along the way and a handful of surprises—one being sweeping views that include Mount Rainier, the Issaquah Alps, and the Olympic Mountains.

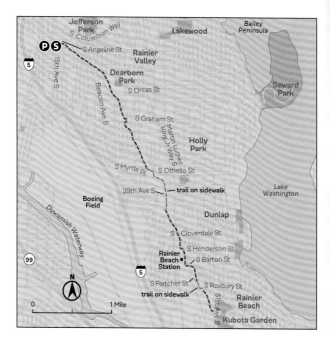

You'll also pass vibrant neighborhoods and some of the most productive P-Patches in the city.

GET MOVING

One of the city's newer long-distance paved trails, the Chief Sealth Trail has yet to make it on many local walkers' and runners' radar screens. The trail connects Beacon Hill to Rainier Beach, traversing primarily neighborhoods and staying clear of busy and noisy commercial areas. Except for the sounds of distant planes taking off and landing, it's a pretty peaceful path. Opened to the public in 2007 through a joint effort of several public agencies, the path was constructed with recycled excavated soils from the nearby light rail line. Since this trail doesn't follow an old railbed, there are some contours

Running the rolling Chief Sealth Trail

to it. Its only flaws are a lack of developed trailhead facilities and a missing midsection that requires a 0.6-mile trek on sidewalks—albeit along very quiet residential streets.

From the S. Angeline Street Trailhead, the path begins its rolling route along a well-maintained green lawn beneath high-tension wires. Soon the way brushes up against the first of several P-Patches along the trail. This one, the Maa Nyei Lai Ndeic (My Mother's Garden) is primarily worked by immigrants from Thailand and Laos. P-Patches are community gardens and allotments. They are not named after peas, but after the Picardo family, who emigrated from southern Italy. The Picardos' farm in Wedgwood became the city's original P-Patch and is one of only two historical farms remaining in the city (the other is located in South Park and was also founded by Italian immigrants).

The trail crosses some quiet roads before reaching Beacon Avenue S. at 0.6 mile. The crossing is flanked by a pair of bicycling angels defying traditional gender colors. The trail crests its highest point before starting a long descent—interrupted by some small uphill sections. Rainier hovers over the urban landscape to the south. At 1.1 miles cross S. Orcas Street near Dearborn Park. At the S. Juneau Street crossing, the trail resumes a little to the east.

At 1.5 miles cross S. Graham Street. The trail continues straight along a driveway access—then heads southeast. At 2.2 miles the trail reaches S. Myrtle Place. It is now necessary to walk sidewalks. Cross S. Myrtle Place and follow S. Holly Park Drive. Then turn right onto 39th Avenue S. At 2.8 miles return to trail. There is a "floating section" of trail off of Kenyon Way S. to the north. You want to continue south.

Pass the 3-acre Thistle P-Patch before coming to Martin Luther King Jr. Way S. at 3.3 miles. Cross the busy arterial and light rail lines (at the pedestrian signal). You are now at the trail's lowest elevation, meaning it's time to climb again. The trail crosses busy S. Henderson Street and heads up. When the way reaches S. Barton Street, turn left and walk the road for a few skips. Then pick up the trail again. After crossing S. Fletcher Street the trail makes a steep descent and diverts for a short way on Marcus Avenue S. and S. Roxbury Street. It then concludes with a climb terminating at S. Gazelle Street near 51st Avenue S. at 4.3 miles. Now head back on a mostly uphill route.

GO FARTHER

Kubota Garden with its beautiful trails is just a short distance from the south trailhead and is well worth the walk to get to it. A path runs along the treed median on Beacon Avenue for about 2.7 miles—although there are a lot of street crossings, making it less than ideal for running. Jefferson Park has a series of well-designed trails, not to mention some incredible views from its location high on Beacon Hill.

8 Lakeridge Park

DISTANCE:	1 mile roundtrip
ELEVATION GAIN:	225 feet
HIGH POINT:	200 feet
DIFFICULTY:	Easy
FITNESS:	Walkers, hikers
FAMILY-FRIENDLY:	Yes
DOG-FRIENDLY:	On leash
AMENITIES:	Benches
CONTACT/MAP:	Seattle Parks and Recreation
GPS:	N47 30.525 W122 14.994
BEFORE YOU GO:	Park is open from 4:00 AM to 11:30 PM

GETTING THERE

Driving: From downtown Seattle, follow I-5 south to exit 161. Turn left on S. Albro Place and then immediately turn right onto Swift Avenue S. Continue for 0.2 mile and turn left onto

A young and curious hiker inspects a ferny maple trunk.

S. Graham Street. Then drive 1.5 miles and turn right onto Rainier Avenue S. Proceed for 3.2 miles, turning right onto 68th Avenue S. Continue 0.2 mile to the trailhead at a hairpin turn (limited parking).

From Renton, take exit 2 on I-405 and follow Rainier Avenue north for 3.7 miles. Turn left on 68th Avenue S. and continue 0.2 mile to the trailhead.

Transit: King County Metro routes 7 and 106 service 64th Avenue S.

Quite possibly the finest forest hike within the Seattle city limits, Lakeridge Park will surprise and impress you. Once a neglected wooded ravine, Lakeridge was revived into a healthy urban wilderness by a dedicated group of volunteers. Follow a wide, well-built, and well-maintained trail up Deadhorse Canyon alongside spring-fed Taylor Creek, beneath a canopy of towering mature trees. You'll feel like you're miles in the backcountry, not minutes from Rainier Beach.

GET MOVING

Located along Seattle's southeastern border, Lakeridge Park is little known to most Emerald City residents. But this 35-acre park has a long, storied past—and a dedicated group of friends that lovingly care for it. From the late 1800s until 1916, Deadhorse Canyon supplied timber for the Taylor Sawmill located downcreek on the shores of Lake Washington. The ravine takes its name either from an ill-fated equine or large fallen unharvested logs referred to by loggers as dead horses.

In 1947 the ravine was deeded to the city, but as a park it languished for the next fifty years, attracting dumping and drug use. In the late 1990s local citizens formed the Friends of Deadhorse Canyon and reclaimed the ravine, replanting it with native vegetation. Today, Deadhorse Canyon contains one of the finest forests in the city.

Follow the trail through the canyon and begin climbing. A set of steps helps with the incline. The trail begins above Taylor Creek—but it can be heard below, drowning out any distant city sounds. Pass some impressive firs, hemlocks, cedars, and maples. Pass too a memorial for Susanna Stodden, who

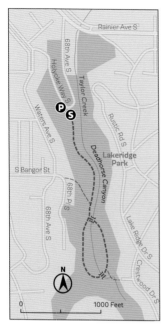

along with her mother was murdered on a trail off of the Mountain Loop Highway in 2006. Stodden was a strong advocate for reviving this canyon.

Pass a couple of long sturdy bridges and a not-so-obvious path heading right. This path climbs steeply to 68th Place S. (no parking), which lies just a couple blocks east of a bus line. The main trail continues up the deep green ravine, coming to a junction. Here the trail makes a loop. You can go in either direction—it makes no difference. The way crosses Taylor Creek two times on good sturdy wooden bridges. Near the upper bridge on the canyon's east side is a side path. Follow it a short way to where it crosses (no bridge) one of the two tributaries making up Taylor Creek. Here you'll find the ruins of an old small-scale sawmill operation. The trail peters out just beyond—so return to the main trail and complete the loop. Then wander back to the trailhead, enjoying this wild little corner of the big city.

GO FARTHER

A mile and a half to the west, located on Renton Avenue S., is Seattle Parks' Kubota Garden. You can spend hours here walking a mile or two on the many paths through these gorgeous 20-acre grounds that blend Japanese garden concepts with

Northwest flora. There are waterfalls, ponds, and a pavilion. The gardens are free to enter, open all year, and great for children. Dogs are allowed on leash.

9 Seward Park

DISTANCE:	About 4.5 miles of trails
ELEVATION GAIN:	160 feet
HIGH POINT:	135 feet
DIFFICULTY:	Easy
FITNESS:	Walkers, runners, hikers
FAMILY-FRIENDLY:	Yes, and paved loop trail is wheelchair and jogger-stroller friendly
DOG-FRIENDLY:	On leash
AMENITIES:	Restrooms, picnic tables and shelters, playground, Seward Park Audubon Center
CONTACT/MAP:	Seward Park Audubon Center
GPS:	N47 33.085 W122 15.401
BEFORE YOU GO:	Park is open from 6:00 AM to 10:00 PM

GETTING THERE

Driving: From downtown Seattle, follow I-5 south to exit 163A (from South King County, follow I-5 north to exit 163). Then continue east on S. Columbian Way for 1.4 miles. Turn right onto Beacon Avenue S. and drive 0.6 mile. Then turn left onto S. Orcas Street and drive 1.6 miles east. Bear right onto Lake Washington Boulevard S. and after 0.2 mile turn left into Seward Park. Continue to parking lots and trailheads along Seward Park Road.

Transit: King County Metro Route 50

Walk or run on a paved path encircling a large peninsula jutting into Lake Washington and be overwhelmed with sublime scenery that includes placid coves, snowy Mount Rainier, tony Mercer Island, and shimmering Seattle skyscrapers rising

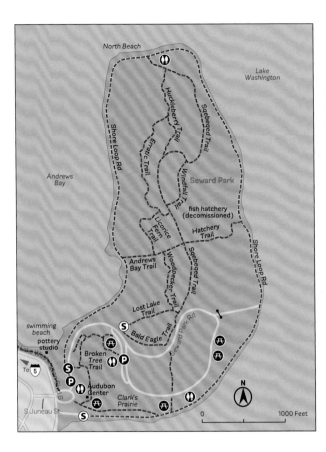

above an emerald Lake Washington shoreline. Then explore the peninsula's interior, following a maze of trails through the city's grandest old-growth forest.

GET MOVING

Acquired in 1911 at what was then an exorbitant price, Lake Washington's Bailey Peninsula was soon transformed into 300-acre Seward Park by the acclaimed Olmsted Brothers (see sidebar "Seattle's Emerald Necklace of Parks"). Named after William H. Seward, who served as secretary of state under Presidents Abraham Lincoln and Andrew Johnson,

SEATTLE'S EMERALD NECKLACE OF PARKS

In April of 1903, renowned landscape architect John Charles Olmsted and his assistant Percy Jones arrived in Seattle to begin designing Seattle parks. The city's population was booming and the City Beautiful movement (emphasizing beautification and monumental grandeur) was in full swing. With the backing of civic leaders, the city hired the Olmsted Brothers landscape architecture firm of Brookline, Massachusetts, to design a world-class parks system.

John Charles Olmsted—the stepson of Frederick Law Olmsted, who designed New York City's Central Park among other famous parks—became the firm's principal designer in Seattle. Upon his initial observation of the area, Olmsted was quoted in the *Seattle Post-Intelligencer* as saying, "I do not know of any place where the natural advantages for parks are better than here. They can be made very attractive, and will be, in time, one of the things that will make Seattle known all over the world."

Olmsted would spend months walking and surveying the city, preparing his master plan, which emphasized a system of parks and parkways preserving "these advantages of water and mountain views and of woodlands, well distributed and conveniently located." He laid it out to include a 20-mile-long system of parks and playfields strung along scenic boulevards. The result was an emerald necklace of parks linked by winding, beautifully landscaped boulevards. As the city grew and annexed other areas, Olmsted expanded his plan, and the city raised levies to help bring it to fruition.

Today, thanks to this emerald necklace of parks, Seattle has one of the most beautifully laid out parks systems of any American city. You can enjoy much of this legacy by hiking, running, and walking many of the parks in this book, including Green Lake, Woodland, Ravenna, Frink, Colman, Mount Baker, Seward, Schmitz, and Lincoln. At Volunteer Park you can witness some of the finest of Olmsted's design principles, and in the park's water tower find interpretive exhibits on the city's parks and Olmsted's legacy.

Seward Park is one of Seattle's crown jewels and contains what the Olmsteds referred to as the Magnificent Forest.

If this is your first visit to Seward Park, spend some time becoming acquainted with the park's many historic structures, which include an old inn-concessionaire that is now the Seward Park Audubon Center.

Run or walk the 2.4-mile perfectly level paved path around the peninsula. This popular trail started as a road and was permanently closed to vehicles in 1971. The path hugs the shoreline the entire way, passing quiet coves, small docks, grassy lawns, inviting beaches, pocket meadows, and spectacular views ranging from mountains to city skyline.

A network of natural-surfaced trails traverses the peninsula's interior—the Magnificent Forest. While not the city's oldest old-growth forest (you'll find that at Schmitz Preserve Park—Trail 3), it's Seattle's largest primeval tract. The Sqebeqed (Lushootseed name for the peninsula) Trail is the most popular and best maintained. It begins near picnic shelter number 3 and travels 1.2 miles across the spine of the peninsula, climbing and dipping along the way to the North Beach. You can spend all day hiking or running by combining the various trails branching off of it. Lots of discovery awaits you with boardwalks, mossy hollows, and arboreal giants.

The Seward Park Audubon Center produces an excellent map (available online) of the park's trails. The center is also a good place to learn about the park's wild denizens, which include bald eagles, mountain beavers, river otters, red-eared turtles, and a feral population of Peruvian conures (parrots). And while evergreen trees dominate your attention in the park, note that Seward supports some Garry oaks as well. Washington's only native oak, it is pretty rare north of the South Sound prairies.

Seward Park's popular Shore Loop Trail

10 Lake Washington Trail

DISTANCE:	3.3 miles one-way
ELEVATION GAIN:	Minimal
HIGH POINT:	25 feet
DIFFICULTY:	Easy
FITNESS:	Walkers, runners
FAMILY-FRIENDLY:	Yes, and paved trail is jogger-stroller friendly
DOG-FRIENDLY:	On leash
AMENITIES:	Restrooms, benches
CONTACT/MAP:	Seattle Parks and Recreation
GPS:	N47 32.991 W122 15.431

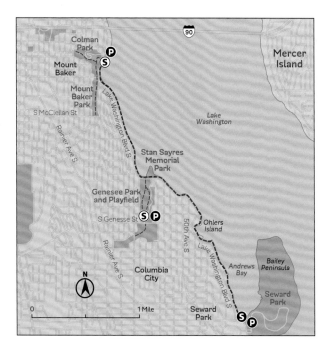

GETTING THERE

Driving: From downtown Seattle, follow I-5 south to exit 163A (from South King County, follow I-5 north to exit 163). Then continue east on S. Columbian Way for 1.4 miles. Turn right onto Beacon Avenue S. and drive 0.6 mile. Then turn left onto S. Orcas Street and drive 1.6 miles east. Bear right onto Lake Washington Boulevard S. and after 0.2 mile turn left into Seward Park. Continue to parking lots and the trailhead.

Transit: King County Metro Route 50

Walk or run on a paved path alongside a treed boulevard and through a ring of parks gracing a mostly undeveloped Lake Washington shoreline. Revel in the beauty of Washington's second-largest natural lake. And marvel at one of the prettiest urban settings in America. Watch boaters, paddlers, swimmers, and waterfowl ply a once foul but now sparkling lake. And catch glimpses of shiny towering buildings and snowcapped mountains, including Washington's grandest peak, Rainier.

GET MOVING

The 9.2-mile-long Lake Washington Boulevard is a legacy of the Olmsted Brothers (see sidebar "Seattle's Emerald Necklace of Parks" in Trail 9). They designed this road and other boulevards in the city to take advantage of the city's landscape, provide views of the lake and distant mountains, and create greenbelts. Lake Washington Boulevard is meant to be traveled slowly to embrace the city's natural beauty. The boulevard is popular with bicyclists, and the 3.3-mile trail running along the boulevard's southern stretch is perfect for pedestrians.

Starting from Seward Park (Trail 9), walk north along the path, passing some Japanese stone lanterns before coming to grassy lawns sloping to the lakeshore. Watch the geese—and

Historic Lake Washington Boulevard bridge in Colman Park

watch your step! The path soon passes a boat ramp and continues along the boulevard and lakeshore beneath a canopy
of mostly eastern and European hardwoods. Plan on returning in autumn for a colorful foliage performance. The trail
winds along a small point near little Ohlers Island (created
when the lake level was lowered in 1916 with the building of the
ship canal). It then passes another boat ramp. Keep walking,
coming to a stretch on a seawall (lakewall?) right along the
lake. Wakes from passing boats occasionally lap the seawall.
At 2 miles come to Stan Sayres Memorial Park, home of the
Mount Baker Rowing and Sailing Center. Just to the south is
Genesee Park with its network of trails.

Next, the trail swings around a cove and continues north
under thick deciduous canopies. Views are great of Bellevue
and the Cascade Mountains across the lake. At 3 miles
reach Mount Baker Beach and a paved path that veers south
through Mount Baker Park. The Lake Washington Trail continues north for another 0.3 mile, terminating at Colman Park.
Here the boulevard turns inland as the lakeshore beyond
sprouts homes. Head back or consider the side trips and
extensions that follow.

GO FARTHER

You can easily extend or vary your run or walk by many miles
by veering off on trails traversing abutting parks. In Genesee
Park you can make a 2-mile loop by following paths across
this large park's meadows and forest patches. The park also
contains a large leash-free area for your four-legged com-
panion. Mount Baker Park has a leafy 0.35-mile paved path
cutting through its ravine. And there's three-quarters of a
mile of peaceful trails (complete with steps) in Colman Park,
including one that leads under several historic Lake Washington Boulevard bridges. This trail terminates (or starts) on 31st
Avenue S. You can access bus lines from all three of these
parks, making one-way walk and run options possible too.

11 I-90 Trail

DISTANCE:	Up to 5.5 miles roundtrip
ELEVATION GAIN:	Up to 300 feet
HIGH POINT:	200 feet
DIFFICULTY:	Easy
FITNESS:	Walkers, runners
FAMILY-FRIENDLY:	Yes, but be aware of heavy bicycle use
DOG-FRIENDLY:	On leash and be aware of bicycles
AMENITIES:	Benches, restrooms, sculptures
CONTACT/MAP:	Seattle Parks and Recreation; Washington State Department of Transportation
GPS:	N47 35.660 W122 18.997

GETTING THERE

Driving: From downtown Seattle, follow E. Yesler Way east for 0.5 mile and turn right onto Boren Avenue. Then immediately bear right onto 12th Avenue S. and drive 0.5 mile. Just after crossing the José Rizal Bridge (12th Avenue bridge), bear right at the intersection, leaving the arterial and continuing on S. Charles Street, which becomes 12th Avenue S. Come to trailhead parking in 0.1 mile at Dr. José Rizal Park.

Transit: King County Metro routes 36 and 60

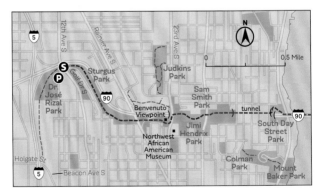

Perhaps the most urban trail of them all, the I-90 Trail is one of the more intriguing and interesting of the lot. Although it is heavily used by bicyclists, a walk on this paved path paralleling I-90 allows a slower pace to take in breathtaking city views and a slew of historical and cultural sites. The trail weaves together a string of parks and traverses the heart of Seattle's historic Italian and African American communities before traveling through a tunnel beneath Mount Baker Ridge and emerging to a stunning view of Lake Washington, the Bellevue skyline, and the I-90 floating bridges.

GET MOVING

While the description given here is from west to east starting at the Dr. José Rizal Park, this trail can be accessed from many other points along the way. Parking can be found at some of the parks and along the streets adjacent to the trail, and several bus lines service arterials crossing the trail. And while the trail parallels one of the busiest stretches of highway in the state, noise barriers, landscaping, and a freeway cap mean you don't see the highway along much of the route. The 4-mile out and back from Rizal Park to Lake Washington makes for a great run or walk, and there are several opportunities to expand your workout.

Dr. José Rizal Park is named after a Filipino nationalist whose writings helped lead the Philippines to rebel against Spain. A national hero, Rizal was executed by the Spanish colonial government in 1896. This park honors him and the large Filipino population of Seattle. Trails and a large off-leash dog park are some of the amenities offered, and the views of Elliott Bay and the Seattle skyline from here are spectacular.

From the parking lot, walk north a short way along 12th Avenue to the traffic light at the intersection with Golf Drive S. Cross the busy arterial and pick up the start of the I-90 Trail, part of the network of trails that makes up the Mountains to Sound Greenway, which extends from Alki Beach to Ellensburg.

I-90 Trail is also part of the Mountains to Sound Greenway.

Soon come to a junction. A paved trail heads left 0.7 mile to Holgate Street. It is best to avoid this path as it is often littered with debris and traverses an area rife with homeless camps.

You want to go right on the I-90 Trail across a well-maintained greenbelt. The first park you come to is Sturgus, providing good views of Seattle's downtown skyline.

Sturgus yields to Daejeon Park, which commemorates Seattle's sister city in South Korea. Take a break to check out the pagoda and view of Mount Rainier framed through its openings, then continue east. A spur veers right to Rainier Avenue S., while the main trail crosses a series of overpasses. Here it brushes up alongside the busy highway it is named for—but only briefly before ducking behind a noise barrier. Enjoy an excellent view of Mount Rainier over the Rainer Valley.

The trail then enters tiny Benvenuto Viewpoint, which sits at the entrance of the I-90 tunnel. Italian for "welcome," *benvenuto* is appropriate given that the surrounding area was once known as Garlic Gulch because of its Italian American population. Many of Seattle's Italian immigrants were drawn (as were many Japanese immigrants) to the Rainier Valley's small farm plots. The I-90 Trail continues east, skirting the southern reaches of the Central District, the historic center of Seattle's African American community.

Now on the freeway lid, come to a junction. The trail straight ahead leads to Judkins Park and Rainier Avenue. You want to carefully cross busy 23rd Avenue S. and enter the new Jimi Hendrix Park, commemorating one of Seattle's most famous sons and legendary Rock and Roll Hall of Famer. The trail passes by the old Colman School, now the Northwest African American Museum (worth a visit). You can walk along some paths lined with purple ribbon sporting Hendrix lyrics. Feel free to kiss the sky while roaming the grounds of this interesting park.

The I-90 Trail continues east, soon coming to Martin Luther King Jr. Way S. Carefully cross it and enter Sam Smith Park, the largest park on the freeway lid. The gorgeous church to your right is the historic Our Lady of Mount Virgin. Once predominantly filled with Italian parishioners, the church now caters to a diverse congregation, including new immigrants from Asia.

The trail winds through Sam Smith Park, passing sculptures, playgrounds, and an off-leash park before entering a tunnel through Mount Baker Ridge. Run or walk through the 0.3-mile lit tunnel, emerging at an overlook above the I-90 floating bridges. Then make a curvy descent. The I-90 Trail continues alongside the westbound I-90 floating bridge. If you want to run or walk this 1.1-mile bridge, consider ear protection as the traffic roar can be deafening. The trail then continues across Mercer Island on its way to Bellevue. You want to instead walk down the adjacent stairway to South Day Street Park (use caution crossing Lakeside Avenue S.), where there is a great view from beneath the bridge (before its floating section of course!). Then turn around and return to your start.

GO FARTHER

For a return variation that'll give you a great stair workout, skip the tunnel and instead go up and over Mount Baker Ridge. Follow S. Atlantic Street or S. Irving Street (utilizing stairways between drivable sections) up the ridge. Be sure to stop at the Mount Baker Ridge Viewpoint Park on 31st Avenue S. for a great view west of the city. Then descend on stairs along the S. Day Street corridor, returning to the I-90 Trail in Sam Smith Park.

You can also extend your trip (easily tacking on another mile) with a walk on the paved trails through Judkins Park. Or from Lake Washington Boulevard S., just above the I-90 Trail tunnel, you can walk south a quiet 0.25 mile to Colman Park and then combine this trip with the Lake Washington Trail (Trail 10). It's 3.9 miles from the I-90 Trail to Seward Park (Trail 9).

12 Frink and Leschi Parks

DISTANCE:	About 2 miles of trails
ELEVATION GAIN:	Up to 300 feet
HIGH POINT:	300 feet
DIFFICULTY:	Easy to moderate
FITNESS:	Walkers, runners, hikers
FAMILY-FRIENDLY:	Yes, but use caution crossing S. Frink Place
DOG-FRIENDLY:	On leash
AMENITIES:	Restrooms
CONTACT/MAP:	Seattle Parks and Recreation
GPS:	N47 36.065 W122 17.123
BEFORE YOU GO:	Park is open from 6:00 AM to 10:00 PM

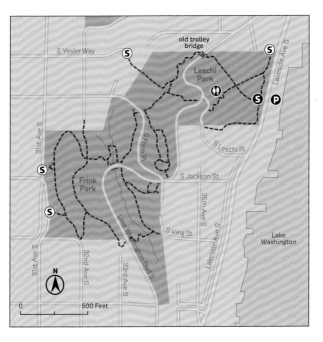

GETTING THERE

Driving: From downtown Seattle, follow E. Yesler Way east for 1.8 miles and turn left on 32nd Avenue S., which soon becomes Lake Dell Avenue. Follow this road, which becomes E. Alder Street, for 0.5 mile to Lake Washington Boulevard. Turn right and follow this road, which soon becomes Lakeside Avenue S., for 0.2 mile to Leschi Park. Park on the street or in the small lot on the east side of the road.

Transit: King County Metro Route 27; for Frink Park, take King County Metro routes 14 and 987 (very limited service)

Explore two little adjoining forested parks packed with trails, history, and surprises. The closest patch of forest to downtown Seattle's steel-and-glass jungle, Frink and Leschi parks offer a touch of wild just minutes from the heart of the city. Explore steep wooded slopes and ravines above Lake Washington. Marvel at a pretty little cascade—and come spring, savor the sights and scents of blossoming rhododendrons.

GET MOVING

Leschi Park has long sported manicured lawns and well-loved tennis courts. But its upper reaches, along with neighboring Frink Park, were for years a tangled and unwelcoming mess of invasive species. It's sad when you consider that these parks were part of the famous Olmsted Brothers' emerald necklace of parks and boulevards (see sidebar "Seattle's Emerald Necklace of Parks" in Trail 9) emphasizing aesthetics, accessibility, and urban livability. But these parks, especially Frink (named for John Frink, president of the Seattle Board of Park Commissioners, who donated these 17 acres to the city in 1906), had become neglected. All that changed with the formation of the citizens group Friends of Frink Park, which revitalized these parks with a top-notch trail system and restoration of native plants.

Lone big cedar in Frink Park

Starting in 18-acre Leschi Park (named for the Nisqually tribe's leader, Chief Leschi, who was executed for murder during a rebellion in 1856, but later exonerated of the crime), catch good Lake Washington views, where ferries once plied this great lake. Then head uphill on wide paths across inviting lawns sporting impressive trees, including some sequoias. Now start your wanderings on the trails. Along the park's northern boundary, walk a path on an old trolley bridge spanning Lake Washington Boulevard. A streetcar once connected

E. Yesler Way to an amusement park at Leschi Park. An even steeper tram via a trestle once climbed the slopes of Frink.

You can walk a steep trail (with lots of steps) up to Yesler to a memorial for prominent Native American activist Bernie Whitebear and his sister Luana, who was a Native American health care administrator, or take another path up to S. Frink Place. Here a path crosses the road, then descends to Lake Washington Boulevard, where a bridge crosses a small waterfall. Another path descends as well, passing big madronas to the ruins of the old caretaker's cottage. Both these trails lead to Frink Park.

Here you can make various loops, which can include some good climbing (complete with steps). Below the waterfall bridge, a path leads along Frink Creek through a glen of rhododendrons. You can then cross the creek and begin climbing along Frink's southern boundary. Cross Lake Washington Boulevard and head up a steep slope. Come to a junction where you can go right to make a shorter loop that passes a wetland seep fed by springs on your way back to the waterfall bridge, or head left and keep going upward. If you take the path to the left, you'll come to an opening that once housed a clay tennis court. Here you can continue straight to a trailhead on 31st Avenue S. (bus stop nearby) or head right, traversing the steep wooded slope. During winter, the predominantly deciduous tree cover here is bare of its foliage, granting peekaboo views of Lake Washington and the Cascades.

Come to another trail junction with a spur leading left and up to 31st Avenue S. Head right and lose all that elevation gained and come to a junction where you can go right to the wetland seep or left to 32nd Avenue S. If you continue straight, you come to the prettiest part of the park. Here you'll pass a big old cedar at a small wetland above a waterfall. The waterfall was designed by the Olmsteds, and it and the nearby road bridge spanning the tumbling creek are quite pleasing to the eye.

A grand loop (of sorts) of the two parks will yield about 1.2 miles—and it's easy to double that by hiking all of the parks' trails with a little section repeating.

13 Washington Park Arboretum

DISTANCE:	About 7 miles of trails
ELEVATION GAIN:	Up to 130 feet
HIGH POINT:	150 feet
DIFFICULTY:	Easy to moderate
FITNESS:	Walkers, runners, hikers
FAMILY-FRIENDLY:	Yes
DOG-FRIENDLY:	On leash
AMENITIES:	Restrooms, interpretive signs, benches, visitors center, Japanese Garden (fee)
CONTACT/MAP:	University of Washington Botanic Gardens
GPS:	N47 38.384 W122 17.681
BEFORE YOU GO:	Park is open from dawn to dusk

GETTING THERE

Driving: From downtown Seattle, follow I-5 north to SR 520. Drive 0.7 mile east and take the first exit (Montlake Boulevard). At the light, proceed straight onto Lake Washington Boulevard E. and drive 0.6 mile, turning left onto E. Foster Island Road. Continue 0.1 mile and then turn right onto Arboretum Drive E. Then immediately turn left into a parking area at the Graham Visitors Center. Additional parking can be found along Foster Island Road and other roads abutting the arboretum.

Transit: King County Metro routes 11, 43, and 980 (very limited service)

A 230-acre emerald wedge of native forest and ornamental gardens, the Washington Park Arboretum offers some of the

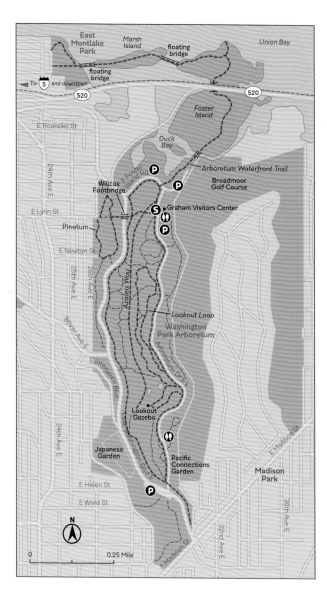

most aesthetically pleasing paths in the city. From islands on Lake Washington to a small ridge, amble, jog, run, or stroll on miles of well-tended trails through acres of well-tended flora. Come in the spring for gorgeous blossoms and in autumn for stunning foliage. And come year-round for peaceful wandering.

GET MOVING

The arboretum consists of several wide main trails and a slew of small connector paths. You can make many return trips, never repeating a previous route taken. If you've come to learn about flora—both native and from other regions—take your time and let discovery be your guide. If you've come for a workout, there are a couple of good loops you can make on the main trails, which include some hills.

Absolutely walk the 0.75-mile Azalea Way in the late spring for one of the finest displays of flowering members of the heath family—rhododendrons and azaleas galore. A former skid road turned racetrack turned blossoming byway, this trail is stunning in May. You can turn this walk into a loop by crossing Lake Washington Boulevard E. and walking trails along the arboretum's western reaches. Before crossing back over via the Willcox Footbridge, walk the half-mile loop through the Pinetum, taking in the sights and fragrances of several species of pines.

The Arboretum was established in 1934 and initially developed by the WPA. Improvements and expansions continue. In 2013 a New Zealand–themed area with new trails was added to the Pacific Connections Garden. And in 2017 a paved 1.2-mile trail paralleling Lake Washington Boulevard E. was opened. This path combined with the paved and closed-to-vehicles Arboretum Drive E. is referred to as the Arboretum Loop (open to bikes). It's 2.5 miles long and includes a good hill climb and a few little dips. The 1.2-mile section of the trail can also be combined with Azalea Way for a 2-mile loop.

Azalea Way

The 1-mile Lookout Loop follows the crest of the small ridge within the park. You can access this trail from many connector trails coming off of the loop or Azalea Way. There's a territorial view of the arboretum from the Lookout Gazebo near the park's high point.

On warm summer days the action at the arboretum is on the Arboretum Waterfront Trail. This 1.1-mile trail leaves from close to the visitors center and heads north along Duck Bay, crossing a bridge to Foster Island and ducking under the busy 520 freeway. The trail then comes to a junction. The path straight ahead leads to a grassy lakeshore spot popular with college students and families. The path to the left heads west on boardwalks and floating bridges to Marsh Island and then to East Montlake Park. Enjoy good views of Union Bay, Husky Stadium, and a flotilla of watercraft. It is a great trail, popular with families and birders, but unfortunately it occasionally floods, and it's in dire need of upgrading and maintenance. Arboretum directors, city leaders, and concerned citizens are currently addressing this need.

GO FARTHER

Admire a totem pole at East Montlake Park before continuing west for 0.5 mile on the Ship Canal Trail. This path heads along the Montlake Cut, which connects Lake Washington to Lake Union. The cut was part of the Lake Washington Ship Canal—built between 1911 and 1934—which aided transportation and commerce between Puget Sound and lakeside communities but consequently lowered Lake Washington by 9 feet. Today the canal is used primarily by pleasure craft. The trail ends in West Montlake Park. You can then follow quiet sidewalks to the Montlake Bridge, where it is a short walk via sidewalk and pedestrian bridge to the Burke-Gilman Trail (Trail 18) on the University of Washington campus. The new SR 520 Trail crossing Lake Washington on a floating bridge can be accessed from the 24th Ave. E. near the cut.

14   Union Bay Natural Area

DISTANCE:	About 1.5 miles of trails
ELEVATION GAIN:	Minimal
HIGH POINT:	30 feet
DIFFICULTY:	Easy
FITNESS:	Walkers, hikers
FAMILY-FRIENDLY:	Yes
DOG-FRIENDLY:	On leash
AMENITIES:	Restrooms (weekdays)
CONTACT/MAP:	University of Washington Botanic Gardens
GPS:	N47 39.508 W122 17.421

GETTING THERE

Driving: From downtown Seattle, follow I-5 north to SR 520. Drive 0.7 mile east and take the first exit (Montlake Boulevard). Turn left onto Montlake Boulevard E. and drive 1.3 miles, merging onto NE 45th Street. Continue east on NE 45th

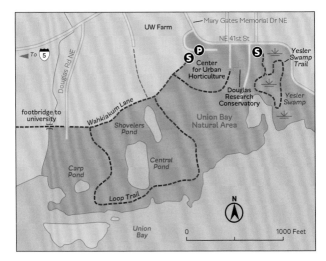

Boardwalk on Yesler Swamp Trail

Street for 0.3 mile. Then turn right onto Mary Gates Memorial Drive NE and drive 0.2 mile. Turn right into the parking area and trailhead at the University of Washington's Center for Urban Horticulture.

Transit: King County Metro Route 78; routes 31, 32, 65, 67, and 75 service NE 45th Street, from where it is a short walk on Mary Gates Memorial Drive NE to trailhead; also accessible via Sound Transit Link light rail, University of Washington Station

One of the best places in the city for birding, the Union Bay Natural Area was once a landfill. You'd have a hard time visualizing that now as cottonwoods, willows, and native grasses and shrubs grace this peaceful spot on Lake Washington's Union Bay. Take to a series of trails across meadows and along wetlands, savoring sweet bird songs and sublime lake views, which include Mount Rainier hovering over the sparkling water.

GET MOVING

When Lake Washington was lowered by 9 feet in 1916 as a result of the Lake Washington Ship Canal, more than 600 acres of land were newly exposed. Union Bay once extended to where the University Village shopping center now stands. This newly exposed area became mostly marsh—then it was filled in, literally paving the way for Husky Stadium, Hec Edmundson Pavilion, student housing, commercial developments, and a landfill.

In 1971, the Montlake Landfill (locally known as The Fill) was capped with clean soil. Over the next several decades (and continuing today), folks from the University of Washington's Center for Urban Horticulture (which manages this property) and countless volunteers have been reclaiming and restoring this 74-acre property. Today it is one of the largest wetlands on Lake Washington and one of the best places in the city for birds.

From the trailhead at the Center for Urban Horticulture, head west on a trail named Wahkiakum Lane. Soon come to a junction with a trail leading east to the Douglas Research Conservatory and the trailhead for the Yesler Swamp Trail. Count on walking it now or upon your return from the natural area's loop trail. The 0.35-mile Yesler Swamp Trail is almost entirely constructed of boardwalks. It makes a loop, complete with observation decks, through the small swamp.

Wahkiakum Lane continues west a short distance before coming to the Loop Trail. Veer left on it and traverse meadows harboring wetland pools and ponds. Scan these wet pockets for turtles and amphibians and look closely among the reeds and grasses for a wide array of birds. More than 150 species have been recorded here, including species uncommon in Western Washington.

The Loop Trail passes benches and approaches Union Bay (stay on the trail to allow for plant restoration), where you get some excellent views across the lake to Mount Rainier and the 520 floating bridge. Highway noise is a constant, but birdsong overpowers it when you focus on the natural surroundings.

When the Loop Trail rejoins Wahkiakum Lane, you can turn right (east) to return to the trailhead or head left and walk a short distance to a small bridge spanning a canal, where it's fun to watch paddling students try to maneuver their canoes beneath the low bridge. The trail ends at a parking lot for the UW's Intramural Activities Building (IMA). If you still want to walk some more, there are a couple of gravel roads (closed to vehicles) veering north off of Wahkiakum Lane.

15 Elliott Bay Trail

DISTANCE:	up to 5.3 miles one-way
ELEVATION GAIN:	Minimal
HIGH POINT:	20 feet
DIFFICULTY:	Easy
FITNESS:	Walkers, runners
FAMILY-FRIENDLY:	Yes, and paved trail is wheelchair and jogger-stroller friendly; heavy bike use
DOG-FRIENDLY:	On leash
AMENITIES:	Restrooms, water, picnic tables, public art
CONTACT/MAP:	Seattle Parks and Recreation; Port of Seattle
GPS:	N47 37.707 W122 22.635
BEFORE YOU GO:	Centennial Park is open from 6:00 AM to 11:00 PM

GETTING THERE
Driving: From points north or south of downtown Seattle, follow I-5 to exit 167 (Mercer Street). Then drive Mercer Street

1.6 miles west. Bear right and continue north on Elliott Avenue W. for 0.4 mile. Then take the exit for the W. Galer Street Flyover and continue for 0.3 mile to Alaskan Way W. Turn right and drive 200 feet under the flyover. Then turn right onto W. Galer Street and continue (road bends left onto 16th Avenue W.) 0.2 mile to trailhead parking.

Alternatively, from downtown, follow SR 99 north and take the Western Avenue exit. Then drive north 0.9 mile on Western Avenue W. to Elliott Avenue W. Continue for 1 mile, then turn right onto the W. Galer Street Flyover and follow the preceding directions.

Transit: King County Metro routes RapidRide D, 19, 24, and 33

Walk or run the Elliott Bay Trail and you'll quickly confirm why Seattle is one of the prettiest cities in North America. From this 5-plus-mile paved path along the heart of Seattle's Puget Sound waterfront, enjoy stunning, sweeping views of the city skyline, Mount Rainier, and the Olympic Mountains forming a jagged backdrop to a vessel-dotted Salish Sea. More than a few Northwest iconic views can be had from this trail.

GET MOVING

While the Elliott Bay Trail is part of a large network of interconnecting bike paths and routes used heavily by commuting cyclists, it should not be ignored by bipeds. The best part of this path for walking and running is the middle 1.6-mile section through shore-hugging Myrtle Edwards and Centennial parks, which includes separate paths for bikes and pedestrians. This section also adjoins the Olympic Sculpture Park, a wonderful place for walking and running as well as admiring some neat pieces of art. And finally, this stretch of trail is one of the absolute best places in the city for sunset strolls.

The trail begins at the Elliott Bay Marina (free parking available, though this is not the suggested start described

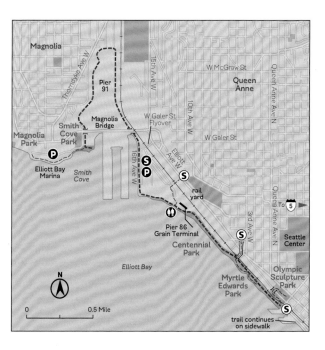

in the driving directions), heading east along Smith Cove to the in-the-making Smith Cove Park. This Seattle city park will eventually have sports fields and courts and a loop path. From here the Elliott Bay Trail bends north, ducking under the Magnolia Bridge and swinging around the massive Pier 91 parking lot. The trail then intersects 21st Avenue W. and bends south, paralleling the pier complex and a large railroad yard. It's not a scenic stretch—but it provides a traffic-free corridor in this busy area.

The trail ducks beneath the Magnolia Bridge again, reaching 16th Avenue W. and parking (and the suggested start). The path then briefly parallels the Smith Cove Waterway before bending left to begin its incredibly scenic shoreline journey along Elliott Bay. Prepare for a visual lovefest. The Seattle skyline shimmers before you. A flotilla of watercraft of all sizes and functions plies the bay in front of you while Mount Rainier provides the perfect backdrop. Now cock your head to the west and soak up a glorious view of the Olympic Mountains across the Sound.

Continue walking or running, soon entering the manicured lawns of the Port of Seattle's Centennial Park and Seattle's Myrtle Edwards Park. When you come to a bait shop, café, and restrooms, the trail splits for bikers and pedestrians. The walking path weaves to the right. Now pass the massive and impressive eleven-story Pier 86 Grain Terminal. Walk beneath the conveyor system that transports tons of grains to large tankers in waiting.

As you continue, you'll find enticing benches, a rose garden, a totem pole, interpretive signs, and a small lighthouse along the way. Pass two paved side trails leading to long overpasses spanning the paralleling railroad tracks and allowing trail access and parking from Elliott Avenue and 3rd Avenue W. The split trail eventually reunites and passes a small closed beach area that often harbors harbor seals (do not approach any marine mammals). Next up come to some interesting sculptures and a couple of side paths leading left to the adjacent Olympic Sculpture Park.

Opened to the public in 2007, this Seattle Art Museum property was once an industrial site. Now you can wander its 9 acres (free and open thirty minutes before sunrise to thirty minutes past sunset), mesmerized by stunning outdoor art and sublime views across the Sound. The Elliott Bay Trail continues, reaching Alaskan Way at 3.5 miles. The trail now advances on a wide sidewalk that passes busy piers. At 3.9 miles (just past the Bell Street pedestrian bridge), a paved trail resumes on the east side of Alaskan Way. Here the trail parallels tracks that once served the George Benson Waterfront Streetcar Line. If this line is ever reinstated it'll give runners and walkers an option of an easier return on this stretch.

Elliott Bay Trail offers excellent views of the Seattle skyline.

From here the trail is quite busy, usually choked with crowds of tourists and workers. To complicate matters, there is ongoing construction of a new SR 99 tunnel and the impending demolition of the Alaskan Way Viaduct. If you decide to keep pushing on, follow this very urban corridor all the way to Colman Dock and Pier 50 at 5.3 miles. Here car ferries depart for Bainbridge Island and Bremerton and passenger ferries head to West Seattle, Vashon Island, and Bremerton. Due to major construction, the trail currently ends here. Eventually it will connect with a bike corridor that continues south to the bike route and trail heading west to Harbor Island and West Seattle.

GO FARTHER

Jump on the passenger ferry to West Seattle and combine this trail with the Alki Trail (Trail 2).

16 Discovery Park

DISTANCE:	More than 12 miles of trails and more than 1.5 miles of beach walking
ELEVATION GAIN:	Up to 500 feet
HIGH POINT:	350 feet
DIFFICULTY:	Easy to moderate
FITNESS:	Walkers, hikers, runners
FAMILY-FRIENDLY:	Yes
DOG-FRIENDLY:	On leash; dogs not permitted on beaches and Wolf Tree Nature Trail
AMENITIES:	Restrooms, water, interpretive signs, benches, Environmental Learning Center, Indian Cultural Center, historic buildings, playfields, picnic tables
CONTACT/MAP:	Seattle Parks and Recreation; map available online (Friends of Discovery Park) and at the Environmental Learning Center
GPS:	N47 39.493 W122 24.363
BEFORE YOU GO:	Park is open from 4:00 AM to 11:30 PM

GETTING THERE

Driving: From downtown Seattle, follow I-5 to exit 167 (Mercer Street). Then drive Mercer Street 1.6 miles west. Bear right and continue north on Elliott Avenue W. for 0.6 mile, which becomes 15th Avenue W. Follow this road for 1.4 miles, then take the Nickerson Street exit. Bear right on W. Nickerson Street (crossing 15th Avenue W.) and then turn left onto W. Emerson Street. Follow for 0.5 mile and turn right onto Gilman Avenue W. Now drive 1 mile (the road becomes W. Government Way in 0.5 mile) to the Discovery Park entrance. Proceed straight 0.1 mile on Discovery Park Boulevard and turn left into the East Parking Lot with access to trails and the Discovery Park Environmental Learning Center. Other main parking areas can be accessed via Texas Way (North Parking Lot), and W. Emerson Street (South Parking Lot).

From Ballard and points north, follow 15th Avenue W. south across the Ballard Bridge to the Nickerson Street exit and head west on W. Emerson Street, following the preceding directions.

Transit: King County Metro Route 33 to access the East Parking Lot; routes 19 and 24 to access the South Parking Lot

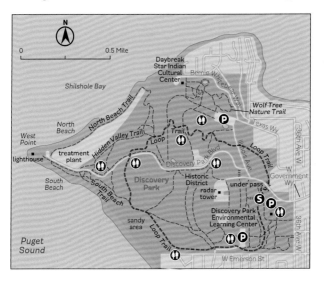

At 534 acres and containing mature forests, towering coastal bluffs, meadows, nearly 2 miles of sandy Puget Sound shoreline, and many historic structures, Discovery Park is Seattle's grand park. It's the place you bring out-of-town guests. And if you live here, it's a place you never tire of visiting. With more than 12 miles of trails and a varied landscape, there's much to discover in Discovery Park.

GET MOVING

Occupying much of the former grounds of Fort Lawton on Magnolia Bluff, Discovery Park has retained several attractive historic buildings and structures from the old army base. Inaugurated in 1900, Lawton was never a major installation, but activities were ramped up at the base during World War II, making it the second-largest port of embarkation for troops headed to the Pacific theater. Lawton housed several thousand German and Italian POWs and was the scene of a riot between Italian POWs and US soldiers, leading to the court-martialing and imprisonment of twenty-eight African American soldiers. In 2007, their convictions were overturned, and the army issued a formal apology for their wrongful convictions.

History buffs will find plenty to their liking here, but so will nature lovers. In 1973 much of the fort became Discovery Park, named for Captain George Vancouver's ship. Today, the park is one of the wildest places within the city, providing habitat for more than 270 species of birds as well as seals, sea lions, and many other mammal species. In 2009 a cougar took up residence in the park but has since been relocated to the Cascades.

Be sure to pick up a map (online or from the Environmental Learning Center) and then consider the options. You can sneak a quick walk in, hike all day, or patch together a challenging trail run. One of the park's most popular options is its 2.8-mile Loop Trail. You can access it from the East and South

Exploring the beach by West Point Lighthouse in Discovery Park

parking lots. This well-maintained and marked National Recreation Trail travels through forested ravines and skirts meadows and the historic district. It also runs along the top of the park's southwest bluffs, granting breathtaking views of Puget Sound. And since it primarily stays on the bluff, there are no big elevation gains and losses.

Many of the park's secondary trails radiate from the Loop Trail, allowing you to extend your hike or run and create longer loops. The 0.7-mile Hidden Valley Trail offers a forested alternative route along the bluff's western edge. The North Beach Trail is my favorite, leading you via steps and a steep descent off the bluff to North Beach. Then it hugs the shore and a lagoon for 0.6 mile to West Point. If the tide is low, you can walk the sprawling sandy beach. Hidden in thick vegetation between the North Beach Trail and Hidden Valley Trail is the West Point Treatment Plant.

At West Point (which can also be driven to by folks with disabilities and groups that include young children—inquire at the Environmental Learning Center for passes) you'll find a small spit, dunes, and an 1881-built lighthouse. It's a place made for lounging on sunny summer days. You can walk nearly a mile on South Beach beneath the southwestern-facing bluffs, or take the South Beach Trail for some good climbing—steps help—and views along its route to the Loop Trail. Consider walking some of the old roads (now trails) and paths through the historic district, where you can marvel at the restored fort buildings.

The Wolf Tree Nature Trail (dogs prohibited) in the northern reaches of the park, near the Daybreak Star Indian Cultural Center, is a quiet path to include in your Discovery Park plans.

A grand loop of the park, incorporating parts of the Loop, North Beach, and South Beach trails is generally around 4.5 to 5 miles and 300 to 400 vertical feet of climbing, depending on your route.

Golden Gardens Park

DISTANCE:	More than 3 miles of trails
ELEVATION GAIN:	Up to 300 feet
HIGH POINT:	300 feet
DIFFICULTY:	Easy to challenging
FITNESS:	Walkers, hikers, runners
FAMILY-FRIENDLY:	Yes
DOG-FRIENDLY:	On leash
AMENITIES:	Restrooms, water, interpretive signs, benches, off-leash park, play equipment, picnic tables
CONTACT/MAP:	Seattle Parks and Recreation
GPS:	N47 41.443 W122 24.150
BEFORE YOU GO:	Park is open from 4:00 AM to 11:30 PM

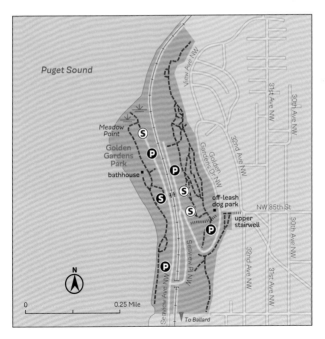

Golden Gardens on a quiet winter day

GETTING THERE

Driving: From I-5, take exit 172 and follow N. 85th Street 3.1 miles west. (Alternatively for less traffic, follow N. 80th Street west to Loyal Way NW.) Then turn right onto 32nd Avenue NW, which quickly becomes Golden Gardens Drive NW and eventually Seaview Place NW. Follow this winding road 0.9

mile to Seaview Avenue NW. Then turn right onto Golden Gardens Park Road and drive a short distance to parking and the trailhead. More parking is available at the upper lot on the east side of the railroad tracks off of Seaview Place.

Transit: King County Metro Route 17X (very limited service); Route 45 stops at stairwell to park at NW 85th Street and 32nd Avenue NW

Golden Gardens Park is one of the finest (and busiest) saltwater beaches in Seattle and one of the best places in the city to catch a sunset, but what most visitors don't realize is that there are some decent trails here too. Definitely walk the paved path along the beach and the nearby nature trail. Then lose the crowds and a few calories by tackling the trails and stairwells on the steep forested bluff above the shore.

GET MOVING

Developed by real estate magnate Harry W. Treat, Golden Gardens Park was meant to lure prospective buyers to new developments in Loyal Heights, Blue Ridge, and Sunset Hill. The park was purchased by the city in 1923, one year after Treat's tragic death in an automobile accident. It didn't take long afterward for this park to become one of the city's crown jewels.

From the trailhead near the beautiful, 1929-built brick bathhouse, head out to Golden Gardens's most famous and valuable asset—its sprawling genuine-sand beach. Here a paved path leads south along the shore for about 0.4 mile to Shilshole Marina (where you can continue along sidewalks). It is an absolutely gorgeous route to run or walk during sunset. Consider visiting in winter when crowds are absent.

North of the bathhouse, a lovely nature trail loops around a marshy meadow and provides access across dunes to more secluded beaches on Meadow Point, and to a small boardwalk across a coastal wetland. This is a good spot to look for birds and marine mammals, and to watch vessels plying the Sound against a backdrop of the snowy Olympic Mountains. This area has been restored to an almost natural state, and it's hard to imagine that it once hosted oil tanks—and a shipyard.

Now if you're looking for a real workout and an escape from the crowds, near the main trailhead locate a pedestrian underpass below the railroad tracks. Head through it and emerge at the upper parking lot, where you can take a trail from the lot, or head for the stairwell to your right. There are some serious stairs in this park, compliments of the WPA and, more recently, Seattle Parks and Recreation. The upper stairwell to 32nd Avenue NW will really get your heart rate up—it's long and steep.

At the top of the lower large stairwell are parking, restrooms, and the popular off-leash dog park. Here you will find a network of trails heading north along a bench on the steep forested bluff. The upper trail travels a little over a half mile through big timber and by some window views out to the Sound. You can make some loops here on these generally quiet trails. There's also an attractive trail that runs on the south side of Golden Gardens Drive. This trail traverses steep slopes and connects to the killer upper stairwell.

Volunteers, students, and parks conservation groups have been working hard lately to eradicate invasive plants from this park. The result is an attractive forest of mature trees and native vegetation close to what Mr. Treat would have seen when he arrived in Seattle in 1903.

GO FARTHER

From the top of the upper stairwell, consider walking 0.6 mile south on 32nd Avenue NW, then west on NW 77th Street to Sunset Hill Park on 34th Avenue NW. This small bluff-top park offers wonderful views of the Sound and mountains—and of course fabulous sunsets as well.

18 Burke-Gilman Trail

DISTANCE:	More than 20 miles one-way
ELEVATION GAIN:	Up to 150 feet
HIGH POINT:	150 feet
DIFFICULTY:	Easy
FITNESS:	Walkers, runners
FAMILY-FRIENDLY:	Yes
DOG-FRIENDLY:	On leash, but be aware of heavy bike use
AMENITIES:	Benches, water, interpretive signs, restrooms (in adjacent parks)
CONTACT/MAP:	Seattle Parks and Recreation; King County Parks
GPS:	N47 41.264 W122 24.107
BEFORE YOU GO:	Trail is not yet complete through Ballard, requiring connecting via streets and sidewalks if you're interested in completing the entire trail in one sweep

GETTING THERE

Driving: The Burke-Gilman can be accessed from several parks (with parking) along its course, including the following: *Golden Gardens Park:* See directions for Trail 17. *Gas Works Park:* From the University District, follow NE Pacific Street west to NE Northlake Way. Drive west on NE Northlake Way for 1 mile to the park. From Fremont, follow N. 34th Street east for 0.2 mile, then turn right onto Stone Way N., which soon becomes N. Northlake Way. Drive 0.4 mile to the park. *Warren G. Magnuson Park:* See directions for Trail 21. *Matthews Beach Park:* From Magnuson Park (NE 74th Street), continue north on Sand Point Way NE for 1.2 miles. Then turn right onto NE 93rd Street and continue 0.1 mile to the park. *Log Boom Park:* From exit 175 on I-5, follow SR 522 (NE 145th Street and then Bothell Way NE) east for 4 miles to Kenmore. Turn right onto 61st Avenue NE, then immediately right onto NE 175th Street, and continue 0.1 mile to the park.

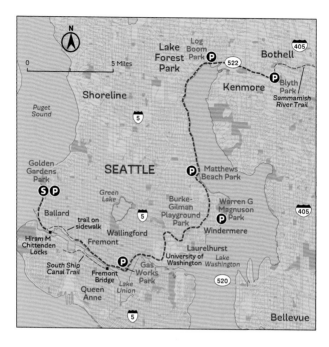

Transit: *Western trailhead at Golden Gardens Park:* King County Metro routes 29 and 44 access trail at Hiram M. Chittenden Locks. *Gas Works Park:* King County Metro routes 31 and 32 stop at N. 35th Street and Wallingford Avenue N., where it is a two-block walk to the park. *Warren G. Magnuson Park:* King County Metro routes 62, 74, and 75. *Matthews Beach Park:* King County Metro Route 75 stops on Sand Point Way NE. *Log Boom Park:* King County Metro routes 309, 312, 331, 342, 372, and 522.

You'll find all walks (and runs and bikes) of life out on the Burke-Gilman, one of the busiest, best-loved rail trails not only in the region but in the country. Traversing several of Seattle's most vibrant neighborhoods and flush with bike commuters, pedestrians, runners, and recreational cyclists, the Burke, as it's commonly referred to by its regular visitors, can get downright crowded at times. The trail runs through or brushes up against some of the city's finest parks—and it offers some of the best views of the city's downtown cluster of glass and steel towers.

GET MOVING

The trail is named after Judge Thomas Burke and Daniel Gilman, two of the main investors who established the original rail line here in 1885—the Seattle, Lake Shore and Eastern Railroad, which was heavily used by logging and coal interests. It was abandoned in 1971, and 12 miles of this line became a rail trail—one of the first in the Northwest—in 1978. The trail has since been expanded by 7 miles, but a 1.4-mile gap still exists in Ballard. However, after more than twenty years of meetings, litigation, negotiations, and assessments, the missing link is scheduled to begin construction in 2018.

Bicyclists are the main users of this trail, although where it traverses the University of Washington campus, pedestrian use is fairly heavy. Long-distance runners like this trail too. Along with the adjoining Sammamish River Trail, it once hosted the Seattle Marathon—and it was on that course back in 1990 that I ran my fastest marathon ever, qualifying me for the Boston Marathon.

Walkers and runners out for shorter workouts will certainly find much of the trail enticing. And when combined with adjoining parks, the trail offers some of the city's most interesting and scenic walks. In general, the western half of the trail is more urban and crowded than the eastern half of the trail, which mostly traverses leafy neighborhoods. What follows is a brief description of the trail from west to east.

The trail starts at the corner of Seaview Avenue NW and Seaview Place NW in Golden Gardens Park. Here it parallels Seaview Avenue NW and an active rail line. Enjoy good views of Shilshole Bay and the Olympic Mountains. The trail eventually crosses Seaview Avenue NW and darts under the railroad, coming to Hiram M. Chittenden Locks (known locally as the Ballard Locks) at 1.8 miles. You can walk on several paved trails on the locks grounds (an engineering marvel) and adjacent Carl S. English Jr. Botanical Garden and Commodore Park. This section makes for a fascinating short walk.

Beyond the locks the trail is currently interrupted for 1.4 miles. The missing link route will eventually parallel NW Market Street and Shilshole Avenue NW to NW 45th Street. If you are intent on continuing to the next section of trail before the new link is built, do not follow that route. Instead opt for a more pedestrian-friendly route along NW Market Street to 11th Avenue NW to NW 45th Street.

At 3.2 miles the trail continues at the corner of 11th Avenue NW and NW 45th Street, passing through an industrial area with little scenic appeal. Use caution at its multiple road crossings. At 4.2 miles the trail (with a parallel gravel section) runs along the treelined Lake Washington Ship Canal in the Fremont neighborhood. This is an exceptionally pretty and busy stretch.

The trail heads through a few high-tech industry campuses and passes beneath the Fremont Bridge at 4.6 miles. Here you can veer off course and walk stairs to the bridge, cross the canal, and run or walk on the much quieter South Ship Canal Trail for 1.5 miles to W. Emerson Place. The Burke-Gilman continues east and is now part of a section of the Cheshiahud Lake Union Loop, which travels for 6 miles around Lake Union along the heavily urbanized lakeshore. While there are some decent running and walking sections on that trail, there are also stretches on sidewalks and along roads.

The Burke-Gilman travels under the Aurora Bridge and past a statue of Sri Chinmoy (a spiritual leader who advocated athleticism—particularly distance running). The trail

Burke-Gilman Trail near Fremont Bridge

then parallels some busy arterials, coming to Gas Works Park at 5.4 miles. Gas Works Park is the site of an old coal-fired power plant (rusty relics still standing). The once-contaminated site has since been transformed into one of Seattle's most loved and iconic parks. Here curvy paths traverse rolling lawns and climb a hill offering stunning views of the Seattle skyline across Lake Union.

The trail continues between busy roads, soon reaching the University District. Here legions of students and University employees join flocks of fitness devotees on the trail. The way travels over 6th Avenue NE and beneath I-5 (Ship Canal Bridge) and Eastlake Avenue (University Bridge). The Cheshiahud Lake Union Loop departs the Burke and heads south along Eastlake Avenue.

At 6.9 miles the Burke-Gilman crosses 15th Avenue NE and proceeds along a busy corridor across the University of Washington campus. Be sure to walk or run in the lane that is separate from bikes here. And feel free to roam the university's beautiful grounds, where miles of well-landscaped paths and stately stairwells will keep you busy for some time.

At 7.3 miles come to a path junction. Here you take a spur to a path leading left to Drumheller Fountain and then right to pedestrian overpasses across busy NE Pacific Place and Montlake Boulevard NE to Husky Stadium. The Burke-Gilman Trail ducks under that overpass and begins angling north. It passes several paths leading to campus buildings and parking lots. It also begins traveling through a more forested and shaded corridor than its western reaches.

The trail crosses Pend Oreille Road NE and darts under NE 45th Street, coming to busy 25th Avenue NE at 8.4 miles. The trail then crosses 30th Avenue NE and comes to a water fountain. It crosses NE 45th Place on an old trestle and continues through residential areas where lots of connector trails lead to neighborhoods.

At 9.2 miles a side trail leads right to the Seattle Children's Hospital. At 9.5 miles the trail crosses 40th Avenue NE and passes through the Burke-Gilman Playground Park (picnic tables and restrooms). It then advances through a cut—one of the few on this trail, passing beneath Princeton Avenue NE. The trail splits twice, with east- and westbound lanes, and continues beneath a lush emerald canopy.

Where the trail abuts the Center for Spiritual Living campus, you'll find signs identifying trailside plants. At 10.7 miles it crosses NE 65th Street, which you can follow east a short distance to Warren G. Magnuson Park. The way then crosses NE 70th Street and NE 77th Street, which you can also walk to Magnuson Park. At 12.6 miles, just after crossing Sand Point Way NE on a bridge, come to Matthews Beach Park—a perfect place for a swim.

The trail then follows close to Lake Washington's shore—but it's lined with homes, so be content with views overlooking backyards. Cross lots of driveways, private ways, and residential roads as the trail travels beneath a bluff alongside the lake. At 16.7 miles it pulls away from the lake and begins to parallel busy SR 522 (Bothell Way NE) in Lake Forest Park, where a slew of restaurants and cafés may entice you to take a break.

The trail continues east along the highway, coming back to lake views and reaching Log Boom Park in Kenmore at 17.5 miles. Beyond, the trail will appeal more to cyclists than pedestrians as it ducks under 68th Avenue NE and parallels SR 522. It now follows along the Sammamish River, reaching the paved Sammamish River Trail at 20 miles just after darting beneath 96th Avenue NE. The Burke-Gilman continues a short distance, crossing the Sammamish River into Blyth Park (parking, restrooms) and ending at 20.6 miles on W. Riverside Drive near 102nd Avenue NE in Bothell.

19 Green Lake and Woodland Parks

DISTANCE:	More than 7 miles of trails
ELEVATION GAIN:	Up to 130 feet
HIGH POINT:	300 feet
DIFFICULTY:	Easy
FITNESS:	Walkers, runners
FAMILY-FRIENDLY:	Yes, and some trails are jogger-stroller friendly
DOG-FRIENDLY:	On leash
AMENITIES:	Restrooms, water, interpretive signs, benches, off-leash park, play equipment, picnic tables, sports fields, swimming pool
CONTACT/MAP:	Seattle Parks and Recreation
GPS:	N47 40.821 W122 19.734
BEFORE YOU GO:	Woodland Park is open from 4:00 AM to 11:30 PM. Parking lots fill fast; consider nearby street parking.

GETTING THERE

Driving: From downtown, follow I-5 north and take exit 170. Then turn left onto NE Ravenna Boulevard and continue 0.5 mile northwest to East Green Lake Drive N. and the main entrance to Green Lake Park.

From North Seattle, follow I-5 south and take exit 171. Then proceed south on 6th Avenue NE and turn right onto NE 71st Street. Now drive west 0.2 mile to East Green Lake Drive N. and the main entrance to Green Lake Park. Alternative parking lots can be found off of West Green Lake Way N. and within adjacent Woodland Park.

Transit: King County Metro routes 26X, 45, 62, and 316; Route 5 goes along west side of Woodland Park

Green Lake Park is quite possibly the busiest, most-loved urban park between Vancouver BC's Stanley Park and Portland's Washington Park. If you have never run, walked, biked,

or inline skated on Green Lake's 2.8-mile paved path that circumnavigates this beloved body of water, then you probably
just moved to town yesterday! There's a longer, soft-surface
path along the park's periphery, and hilly forested trails in
adjacent Woodland Park to offer a little more variety—and
breathing room.

GET MOVING

If you want to feel the pulse of this city, visit Green Lake Park
and find every walk of life Seattle harbors any time of day,
any time of the year. This park is the center of the city's running scene—its oldest specialty running store is just a sprint
from the main parking lot. When I lived in Seattle's Ballard
neighborhood, I ran in this park several days a week. Once

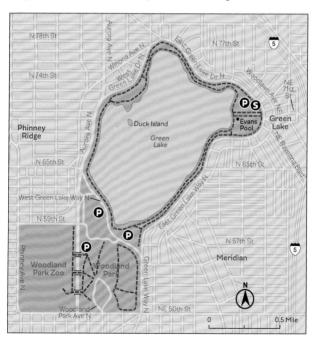

while training for the Boston Marathon, I ran the inner loop eight times, but there was plenty going on around me to keep me entertained.

Glacier-formed and shrunk by development over the years, the 259-acre lake (that now lacks an inlet and outlet creek) became part of the city's grand scheme of parks in 1903 at the behest of the Olmsted Brothers. The most popular path is a 2.8-mile paved trail that circles the lake and hugs its shoreline. It is divided for pedestrian and wheeled travel and can be downright crowded on a hot summer's day. Consider checking it out on a cold rainy day and you'll be surprised at some of the sights. The park teems with ornamental trees, mostly stately eastern hardwoods, but some redwoods and bald cypress trees as well. There are always hundreds— perhaps thousands—of widgeons, coots, and geese at the park too, so watch your step!

A far less used, mostly soft-surface 3.2-mile trail runs along the park's periphery. While it is near busy roads, it passes through some attractive groves of trees, including Japanese cherries. The views are great from both trails, with the Seattle skyline and Mount Rainier visible across the lake from the park's northern reaches.

If you're looking for a good hill workout, head over to adjacent Woodland Park. Although the park is known primarily for its zoo, the eastern half is laced with wide rolling trails through groves of big trees and small meadows. Woodland Park often hosts cross-country meets of various levels, with some being open to the public. If you run the periphery of the park, it's about 1.6 miles. You can easily double or triple that by taking to the connecting trails and darting across the pedestrian bridges over Aurora Avenue and back. The relief in Woodland Park is more than 120 vertical feet, with lots of dips—so have at it, burning some calories before settling in to one of the area's great brewpubs, coffee shops, or eateries afterward.

Rare quiet day at Green Lake

GO FARTHER

Being mindful of street crossings, you can run or walk the greenbelt of Ravenna Boulevard, reaching Cowen Park (Trail 20) in 0.8 mile.

20 Cowen and Ravenna Parks

DISTANCE:	More than 4 miles of trails
ELEVATION GAIN:	Up to 120 feet
HIGH POINT:	200 feet
DIFFICULTY:	Easy
FITNESS:	Walkers, runners, hikers
FAMILY-FRIENDLY:	Yes, and main trail is jogger-stroller friendly
DOG-FRIENDLY:	On leash
AMENITIES:	Restrooms, water, interpretive signs, benches, play equipment, picnic tables, sports fields
CONTACT/MAP:	Seattle Parks and Recreation
GPS:	N47 40.167 W122 18.220
BEFORE YOU GO:	Park is open from 6:00 AM to 10:00 PM; small parking lot at Ravenna Park, but plenty of nearby street parking available

GETTING THERE

Driving: From downtown Seattle, follow I-5 north and take exit 170. Then turn right onto NE Ravenna Boulevard and continue 0.9 mile to Ravenna Park and parking at junction with NE 58th Street.

From North Seattle, follow I-5 south and take exit 171. Then proceed south on 6th Avenue NE and turn left onto NE 70th Street. Drive east 0.2 mile and turn right onto Roosevelt Way NE. Proceed 0.5 mile and turn left onto NE Ravenna Boulevard. Continue 0.7 mile to Ravenna Park and parking, following the preceding directions. Additional parking can be found at a lot at the junction of 20th Avenue NE and NE 58th Street.

Transit: King County Metro routes 45, 71, 73, 74, 372X, and 373X

Explore a 100-foot-deep, thickly forested ravine just minutes from the busy University District. Follow alongside a babbling creek, pass a few big trees (including some non-native incense

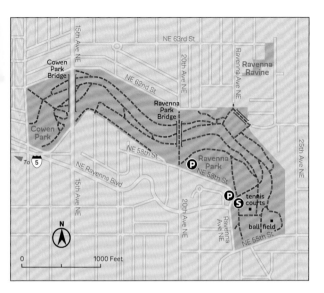

cedars and redwoods), and cruise beneath two historic bridges. While these two adjoining parks are only a mere 57 acres in size, more than 4 miles of trails traverse the half-mile-long ravine they encompass, allowing for long runs and walks.

GET MOVING

Due to their proximity to the University of Washington, expect to see lots of college students running and hiking Ravenna and Cowen parks. Expect lots of families too from the surrounding neighborhoods. And unfortunately, expect to see quite a few homeless encampments too. The park is safe; just be alert for drug paraphernalia and unsanitary waste.

Ravenna is one of Seattle's oldest parks, and it once contained some of the largest and oldest trees remaining in the city. But a mere two years after the city acquired the park from its private owners in 1911, the biggest tree mysteriously disappeared (was cut down). Investigations later showed that

Spring-fed creek at Ravenna Park

a corrupt city parks superintendent (imagine that, a corrupt politician) profited from it. Over the next two decades the other big trees were cut down for various reasons. Despite the loss of these trees, the park still contains plenty of natural allure. It also has lots of historical interest and has been the setting for a couple of novels and a popular comic book series.

From Ravenna's east end near a playground and tennis courts, check out a newly daylighted area of Ravenna Creek, then head up the ravine. A wide service-road trail travels right up the center of the ravine, often alongside the creek, which was once fed by Green Lake. Now it is fed by runoff, and several springs still flow into it. Follow the main trail beneath two historic bridges, first the Ravenna Park Bridge, then the Cowen Park Bridge. The latter is a 1936 WPA-built concrete art deco structure. The former is a 1913-built steel lattice-arched bridge.

Shortly after passing beneath the second bridge, the trail climbs up and out of the ravine to Cowen Park (and its play equipment). To return, take one of the paralleling trails that traverse the ravine's slopes. Combine these trails with several of the paths that climb out of the ravine to neighboring city streets. Then either head back on them or walk a few blocks here and there to create some loops. Be sure to walk or run across the Ravenna Park Bridge. Closed to traffic, the 354-foot-long historic bridge offers views down into the ravine.

21　Warren G. Magnuson Park

DISTANCE:	More than 4 miles of trails
ELEVATION GAIN:	Up to 50 feet
HIGH POINT:	50 feet
DIFFICULTY:	Easy
FITNESS:	Walkers, hikers, runners
FAMILY-FRIENDLY:	Yes, and jogger-stroller friendly
DOG-FRIENDLY:	On-leash and off-leash areas
AMENITIES:	Restrooms, water, interpretive signs, benches, play equipment, sports fields, historic buildings, community garden, sculptures
CONTACT/MAP:	Seattle Parks and Recreation; map available online
GPS:	N47 40.924 W122 15.489

GETTING THERE

Driving: From downtown Seattle, follow I-5 north to exit 168B. Then drive SR 520 east and take the first exit (Montlake Boulevard). Turn left and follow Montlake Boulevard NE (SR 513). At 1.2 miles bear right and follow NE 45th Street west. After 0.5 mile the arterial bends left and becomes Sand Point Way NE. Continue on Sand Point Way NE (SR 513) for 2 miles, then turn right into Magnuson Park at NE 74th Street. Drive 0.3 mile east to a large parking area and trailhead. Alternative parking and trailheads can be reached off of NE 65th Street.

Transit: King County Metro routes 62, 74, and 75

Seattle's second-largest park, Magnuson—like Discovery, Seattle's largest park—owes its existence to the military, and to enlightened civic leaders and citizens who fought for its establishment. Within this park's 350 acres is a whole heck of a lot of history and natural beauty. Check out historic buildings, a large restored wetland, and a spectacular stretch of Lake Washington shoreline. And if you have a four-legged hiker with you, head to the large off-leash area and trail leading down to an off-leash beach.

GET MOVING

Magnuson Park occupies much of a broad peninsula on Lake Washington known as Sand Point. From 1920 to 1970 Sand Point was the home of a Naval Air Station that during its peak in World War II housed 5600 naval personnel and more than 2400 civilians. Upon the base's closure, several factions contentiously fought over the future of this prime property. Thankfully the bulk of the former base became the park it is today. It was named in honor of longtime Washington senator (and former naval officer) Warren Magnuson, who was instrumental in securing the land as a park.

The western and northern reaches of the park have remained developed, containing historic buildings and newer sports fields and courts. Most of the buildings have been refurbished as student housing, community centers, and offices for nonprofits. The park's historic district is definitely worth strolling through. The Mountaineers Seattle Program Center is located in the northwest corner of the park, where you'll also find their public outdoor climbing wall.

The park's eastern reaches are more natural and include a large wetland complex. The wetlands, however, are manmade, occupying parts of the former airstrip, a parking lot, and the site of a large hangar. Today this area is one of the richest bird habitats in the city. Take the trails that traverse it early or late in the day, binoculars and bird guide in hand, and see how many species you can identify.

If you're looking for longer paths to walk or run, head off north or east from the wetlands. Follow the Frog Pond Trail

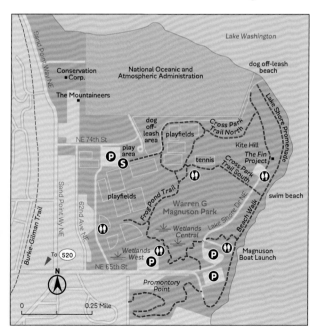

Magnuson Park's Cross Park Trail North

north to either the Cross Park North or Cross Park South trails. Then follow the wide, paved Beach Walk south back to the wetlands. Depending on the wetland route you choose, this arrangement makes for about a 1.5-mile loop.

To the south of the park's boat launch is Promontory Point, which also has a few paths and the park's only real elevation gain (sure, there is a little bump at Kite Hill in the northern reaches of the park). Views of the lake and Cascades are good from here and all along the Beach Walk.

Dogs and their owners have a half-mile leash-free trail from the off-leash play area to the off-leash beach. And speaking of beaches, the lake has a nice one for humans too, making Magnuson a great place to go for a run on a hot summer day with a refreshing cooldown at the end. And whether you visit the park for the first time or come here regularly, you will enjoy the various sculptures in the park. *The Fin Project* is one of the more intriguing. It's a series of dive fins from former submarines, arranged to look like an orca pod. Seattle's famous *Sound Garden* is in the park too. It's the inspiration behind the name for the late Chris Cornell's band, Soundgarden—and today stands as a memorial to the singer, who died in 2017.

Magnuson Park is a favorite spot for group runs and races. So consider signing up for one and meet some new friends.

22 Carkeek Park

DISTANCE:	6 miles of trails
ELEVATION GAIN:	Up to 400 feet
HIGH POINT:	290 feet
DIFFICULTY:	Easy to moderate
FITNESS:	Walkers, runners, hikers
FAMILY-FRIENDLY:	Yes, and some trails are jogger-stroller friendly
DOG-FRIENDLY:	On leash

AMENITIES: Restrooms, water, interpretive signs, benches,
               play equipment, picnic tables, Environmental
               Learning Center
CONTACT/MAP: Seattle Parks and Recreation
GPS: N47 42.698 W122 22.531
BEFORE YOU GO: Park is open from 6:00 AM to 10:00 PM

GETTING THERE

Driving: From exit 173 on I-5, follow N. Northgate Way west
for 0.8 mile to the junction with Aurora Avenue N. (SR 99).
Continue west, now on N. 105th Street for 0.5 mile to the junction with Greenwood Avenue N. Then continue southwest onto
Holman Road NW for 0.3 mile. Turn right onto 3rd Avenue
NW and proceed for 0.4 mile. Turn left onto NW 110th Street
(signed for Carkeek Park) and follow this road, which turns
into NW Carkeek Park Road, for 0.6 mile to the park entrance

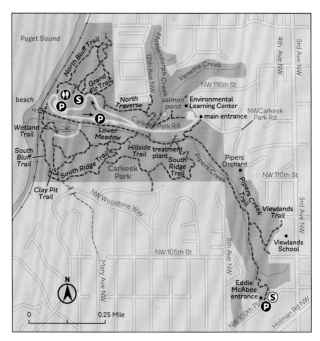

on your left. Enter the park and continue to parking areas and spaces all along the park loop road.

Transit: King County Metro routes RapidRide D and 28X stop at (and Route 40 stops near) Eddie McAbee park entrance on NW 100th Place

A beloved park in North Seattle, Carkeek contains a mile-long forested ravine cradling a salmon-rearing creek; a historic apple orchard; groves of big firs, maples, and cottonwoods; a rich marsh; sandy beach on Puget Sound; and 6 miles of trails. Get a good workout hiking trails complete with steps up and down the ravine's steep forested slopes. Stroll along Pipers Creek savoring sweet water music—or amble along a small sandy spit, mesmerized by the sun setting behind the serrated Olympic Mountains summits.

GET MOVING

At more than 220 acres and containing 6 miles of trails, Carkeek is a park you can easily spend all day exploring. The park was first established in the late 1920s and had the distinction of growing vegetables for feeding animals at the Woodland Park Zoo. In the 1930s, work crews with the Civilian Conservation Corps (CCC) and WPA developed many of the park's trails as well as a few of its structures. During the 1940s, the park briefly housed US Army personnel, and in the 1950s, a sewage-pumping station was constructed within the park. Despite all this activity, the park remains remarkably wild and is one of the better places in the city for a nature walk.

Perhaps the most popular trail within the park is the nearly one-mile-long Pipers Creek Trail. From the Lower Meadow, follow this wide trail upstream along the salmon-rearing creek. There are plenty of good observation points for watching these iconic Northwest fishes. The trail crosses the creek and then swings around the wastewater-pumping plant before crossing the creek again. It then begins to climb out

Hiker admires a bigleaf maple.

of the ravine. Pass an old orchard (since restored after being "rediscovered" in the 1980s) that was used by the Pipers who homesteaded here in the 1880s. The trail continues along the creek, eventually switchbacking to its rim at the Eddie McAbee park entrance on NW 100th Place (bus access and limited parking). Now follow the trail downhill. If you're looking for a workout diversion, take the Viewlands Trail, which climbs steeply with the help of steps to the Viewlands School more than 100 feet above the ravine bottom.

Back near the pumping station you can opt to loop back to the Lower Meadow by following the South Ridge Trail to a series of trails returning to the meadow. The South Ridge Trail climbs out of the ravine then makes a few ups and downs traversing steep slopes. It passes through an attractive forest containing several large maples.

Near its junction with the South Bluff Trail (which offers some window views out over the Sound) is a trail that leads south out of the park, passing under NW Woodbine Way and terminating at NW 105th Street (no parking). At the west end of the Lower Meadow, follow the Wetland Trail on boardwalks through a marsh. Here Pipers Creek continues under railroad tracks to reach the Sound. There is no beach access here. To reach the beach, head to the upper parking lots. Here you'll find a railroad overpass and a set of stairs to the beach and small spit.

North of the salmon-themed playground, which children will love, find another batch of good interconnecting trails. Follow the North Bluff Trail to the North Meadow for a good uphill workout and some decent but limited views of the Sound. The Grand Fir Trail passes some grand firs and a few decent Doug firs. The 12th Avenue Hillclimb will give you a good short workout. And at the park's center you'll find a couple of trails leading to the Environmental Learning Center (closed to visitors), which hosts school programs throughout the year.

23 # Interurban Trail (North)

DISTANCE:	4.4 miles of trail
ELEVATION GAIN:	Up to 300 feet
HIGH POINT:	475 feet
DIFFICULTY:	Easy
FITNESS:	Walkers, runners
FAMILY-FRIENDLY:	Yes, and jogger-stroller friendly
DOG-FRIENDLY:	On leash
AMENITIES:	Interpretive signs, benches, water, restrooms at Echo Lake Park
CONTACT/MAP:	Shoreline Parks, Recreation and Cultural Services
GPS:	N47 44.050 W122 20.872
BEFORE YOU GO:	Be aware that the trail is noncontiguous, with two separate (Seattle and Shoreline) sections

GETTING THERE

Driving to Linden Avenue N.: From exit 175 on I-5, follow N. 145th Street (SR 523) west for 0.9 mile to the junction with Aurora Avenue N. (SR 99). Turn left onto Aurora Avenue N. and after 0.1 mile turn right onto N. 143rd Street. Drive 0.1 mile and turn right onto Linden Avenue N. Park on the road and walk north to N. 145th Street.

Driving to Echo Lake Park: Take exit 177 on I-5 and drive west on NE 205th Street (SR 104) for 0.8 mile. Turn left onto Meridian Avenue N. and drive for 0.2 mile south. Then turn right onto N. 200th Street and proceed 0.25 mile, turning left onto Ashworth Avenue N. Then immediately turn right into Echo Lake Park.

Transit: King County Metro routes 28X and 304 serve N. 145th Street; Route 331 serves Echo Lake Park; several routes serve Aurora Avenue N. in Shoreline

Not as well-known as its southern counterpart (Trail 38), the Interurban Trail (North) traverses the city of Shoreline north

Woods near Interurban Trail's northern terminus

to south with a separate section slicing through a touch of North Seattle. Run or walk part or all of this trail, which follows the corridor of a trolley line that once connected Seattle to Everett from 1910 to 1939. Much of the way is pretty urban, paralleling busy Aurora Avenue, but there's a quiet stretch along Echo Lake and the Evergreen Washelli cemetery that makes for pleasant strolling.

GET MOVING

Shoreline Section: Walk to N. 145th Street (which is the border between Seattle and Shoreline) and find a replica train-depot stop and a kiosk with historic displays. Admire the railroad-lantern-themed mileposts along the way. The route heads north on a slightly downhill course, coming to a pair of elaborate pedestrian bridges spanning busy N. 155th Street and Aurora Avenue. Hit the steps or take to the ramps for gentler climbing and descending.

The path then scoots behind businesses and crosses a few quiet streets. Pass by a handful of coffee shops and restaurants tempting you to break stride. Benches line the trail, and the one at small Darnell Park is a quiet place to catch your breath. Pass a Sephardic Jewish cemetery—the Seattle area is home to one of America's largest Sephardic Jewish communities.

At about 1.5 miles reach N. 175th Street and Shoreline's "downtown." Pass city hall and then walk through a park wedged between busy roads. Here enjoy sculptures and a bricked section of the old Highway 99. The trail reaches N. 185th Street (with compass bearings in the sidewalk), where you'll want to head right a short distance before crossing N. 185th and resuming your walk or run on a paved path.

The way passes a few more side streets before brushing alongside quiet Echo Lake. At about 2.8 miles, reach Echo Lake Park (at the junction of N. 200th Street and

Ashworth Avenue N.). Here find restrooms, parking (for the alternative start), and benches for kicking back and watching the residential waterfowl. This is a good place to turn around, as the trail beyond no longer follows the original trolley line.

If you want to continue, however, walk east on sidewalks along N. 200th Street for 0.3 mile to Meridian Avenue N. Cross this road and enter the grounds of the Ballinger Commons Apartments. Here a paved path heads south—and the Interurban Trail continues north, descending through a wooded tract and reaching NE 205th Street (SR 104) in 0.3 mile. There isn't any parking here, but the trail is serviced by Snohomish County Community Transit Route 416. The trail resumes again in Snohomish County from the Mathay-Ballinger Park.

Seattle Section: Walk a pleasant three-quarter mile or so down Linden Avenue N., passing the Bitter Lake Reservoir Open Space and

Bitter Lake Playfield (both contain short paths), to N. 128th Street. Here the Interurban Trail begins again. After crossing N. 125th Street (use caution), the trail utilizes a quiet corridor between a residential neighborhood and the forested grounds of the Evergreen Washelli cemetery.

Watch for "flip-books" lining the way. This series of successive signs replicates animated flip-books. Bicyclists traveling at a good clip will see the animation. Pedestrians? Try running fast! At 0.9 mile from N. 128th Street, the trail ends on N. 110th Street near its junction with Fremont Avenue N.

24 Boeing Creek Park (Shoreline)

DISTANCE:	3 miles of trails
ELEVATION GAIN:	Up to 275 feet
HIGH POINT:	470 feet
DIFFICULTY:	Easy to moderate
FITNESS:	Walkers, runners, hikers
FAMILY-FRIENDLY:	Yes, and some trails are jogger-stroller friendly
DOG-FRIENDLY:	On-leash trails and off-leash park
AMENITIES:	Interpretive signs, benches, restrooms at Shoreview Park
CONTACT/MAP:	Shoreline Parks, Recreation and Cultural Services
GPS:	N47 45.346 W122 21.681

GETTING THERE

Driving: From exit 176 on I-5, head west on N. 175th Street for 3.9 miles, crossing Aurora Avenue N. (SR 99). Turn left onto Fremont Avenue N. and proceed for 0.1 mile, then turn right onto N. 172nd and drive for 0.1 mile. Next, turn left onto Dayton Avenue N. and continue for 0.3 mile. Now turn right onto Carlyle Hall Road NW, which eventually becomes 3rd Avenue

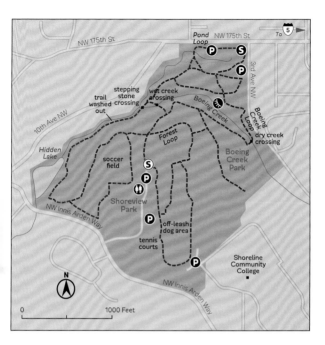

NW, and drive for 0.4 mile to the trailhead. Park on the road. Additional parking can be found on nearby NW 175th Street. Alternatively, you can park and start from Shoreview Park, located off of NW Innis Arden Way.

Transit: King County Metro routes 5, 304, 330, 331, and 345 all service Shoreline Community College

Explore a deep ravine cut by a small creek feeding into a small pond. Admire some of the biggest and oldest trees remaining between Seattle and Everett. And if you're looking for an easy forest walk or a good trail-running workout, you'll find it here. Once part of Bill Boeing's (yes of airplane fame) estate, this park is now the pride of Shoreline.

Cascading Boeing Creek

GET MOVING

Boeing Creek Park borders Shoreview Park and Shoreline Community College—its buildings hidden by a buffer of greenery. The two parks are just shy of 90 acres, making them one of Shoreline's largest greenbelts. And while an excellent trail system threads them together, they offer two different ambiences. At Shoreview Park you'll find sports fields, tennis courts, and cleared land riddled with invasive species, while at Boeing Creek Park you'll find mainly mature forest, including some remnant old-growth giants, and a beautiful cascading creek cutting through a deep gorge.

Study the map and then set out for discovery. There are several signed loops within the parks, and you can easily tie a bunch together, making for a decent run or half-day hike. The Pond Loop is a little over 0.25 mile, and it can be negotiated by a wheelchair or stroller. This wide, level path circles a retention pond. Be sure to read the panels along the way recapping the great New Year's Eve flood of 1996 and its destruction.

The Boeing Creek Loop follows a 0.7-mile loop around the ravine cradling Boeing Creek and includes a good overlook. The trail makes a dry upper-creek crossing (hop rocks to cross) and a wet lower-creek crossing (your tootsies will probably get wet). It also passes some of the park's and Shoreline's biggest and oldest trees. The lower part has suffered some flood damage, so there's a steep reroute where the creek took out the trail.

The Forest Loop is just shy of 0.6 mile, and it can be reached via the Hidden Lake Loop or a connector trail off of the Boeing Creek Loop or from Shoreview Park. It travels through a beautiful, mostly uniform forest of mature second-growth Douglas firs. There's also some elevation gain on this one if you want to burn some extra calories.

The most interesting trail in the park, the Hidden Lake Loop, is officially closed in places due to flooding, but folks do the loop nevertheless. You can easily reach Hidden Lake from Shoreview Park. The little lake was built by the Boeing Company's founder, William E. Boeing, in the 1920s by damming the creek. He used much of this area as a hunting and fishing retreat. In the 1960s he transferred the land to Shoreline to be used for schools, but instead it eventually became the city's flagship park.

Beyond the lake, the trail follows right alongside the cascading creek. It is washed out in places, requiring some steep scrambling on unstable banks or some wading and rock hopping in the creek. The portion of the loop along the ravine's rim is in good shape and allows access to other trails, some of which are unnamed but deserve to be checked out. One branches off from the Forest Loop, climbing a small ridge to a window view of Puget Sound. It then skirts the large off-leash dog area, eventually connecting back with the Forest Loop.

25 Hamlin Park (Shoreline)

DISTANCE:	About 5 miles of trails
ELEVATION GAIN:	Up to 300 feet
HIGH POINT:	450 feet
DIFFICULTY:	Easy
FITNESS:	Walkers, runners
FAMILY-FRIENDLY:	Yes
DOG-FRIENDLY:	On leash
AMENITIES:	Benches, restrooms, playfields, orienteering course
CONTACT/MAP:	Shoreline Parks, Recreation and Cultural Services; map available online from the Cascade Orienteering Club (http://cascadeoc.org)
GPS:	N47 44.713 W122 18.467

GETTING THERE

Driving: From northbound I-5, take exit 175 and drive east on NE 145th Street (SR 523) for 0.5 mile. Then turn left onto 15th Avenue NE and drive 0.8 mile. Turn right onto Hamlin Park Road and continue 0.2 mile to parking and the trailhead.

From Shoreline, take exit 176 from southbound I-5 and drive east on NE 175th Street for 0.8 mile. Then turn right onto 15th Avenue NE and drive 0.7 mile. Turn left onto Hamlin Park Road.

Transit: King County Metro routes 77X and 348

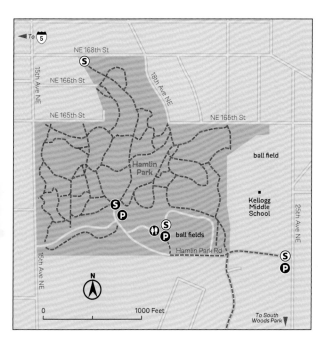

A well-loved park with a long history, Hamlin consists of thick, towering timber, a couple of small ravines, a picnic area and small playfield, and a spaghetti heap of trails. There are trails both official and bootleg crisscrossing nearly every acre of this 80-acre greenbelt. You can download a map—but it'll still be confusing to figure out the trail system. So hike, walk, or run willy-nilly, using your GPS or watch to monitor your required distance or time on the trail.

GET MOVING

Hamlin Park is very popular with area runners. Its generally smooth trails and gentle terrain make it a good choice for runners shunning pavement but not desiring hard-core trails. With its mishmash of trails and proximity to South Woods Park

Long set of steps in Hamlin Park

(and more trails), you can easily run or walk 5 miles without too much repeating. Many of the park's trails were user built, with little regard to environmental sensibilities. The Shoreline Parks Department has recently upgraded some trails and closed some areas for revegetation and is assessing new closures and upgrades. Expect some changes to the trail system here in the future.

The land that the park sits on and near has a long history. It was homesteaded by the Hamlin family in the late 1800s before the navy purchased it in 1923. The navy then constructed a hospital and housing units on the southern part of the homestead, which after World War II became a tuberculosis sanitarium. In the 1960s an eastern section of the property was used for school construction. Most of the northern, primarily forested tract became Hamlin Park. In 2007 a 16-acre section south of adjacent Shorecrest High School was saved from development and became the South Woods Park. While much of the forest cover is fairly uniform, consisting of Douglas fir, there are quite a few western white pines in the park's northwestern reaches.

From the parking area, dirt paths take off north and west while paved paths take off east and west. The Cascade Orienteering Club's map shows all the paths, the main ones depicted darker. If you're into orienteering, check out the course. Otherwise have fun exploring the trails. In the park's northeast corner there is a small ridge that is negotiated by steps, offering an opportunity for some conditioning. The terrain includes lots of dips, allowing you to gain some elevation if you circle around a few times. Area schools use the park for cross-country meets. Consider running their marked courses after they have competed. It's about 1.6 miles if you follow trails around the park's northern periphery. Several trails lead to roads and neighborhoods along the park's northern and western boundaries, so you may be doing some backtracking.

You can also run or walk east on a 0.4-mile paved path leading over a knoll to a parking area on 25th Avenue NE. When school is out of session, follow a 0.4-mile paved path south to Shorecrest High School and then explore the South Woods. Here a short paved path bisects the park, reaching NE 150th Street, while a 0.4-mile dirt path circles around the sloped property.

Next page: *Old quarry now covered in greenery at Maury Island Marine Park*

VASHON AND BLAKE ISLANDS

Consisting of 37 square miles, Vashon Island and adjoining Maury Island make up the largest island in Puget Sound south of Admiralty Inlet. Located a mere 3 miles from Seattle, and only 1.5 miles from Tacoma, Vashon Island couldn't offer a more pronounced contrast to Washington's largest and third-largest cities. Vashon Island and Maury Island (which was connected to Vashon by a manmade isthmus in 1916) are predominantly rural. No bridges (just Washington State Ferries) connect Vashon to the mainland (at Fauntleroy, West Seattle; Point Defiance, Tacoma; and Southworth, Kitsap Peninsula), helping to keep this island a pastoral haven.

Vashon Island is home to less than 11,000 people. There's a small island center, but you won't find many commercial establishments there or throughout the island. What you will find here is a rolling, forested countryside dotted with small farms, tidy homes, a couple of quaint villages, placid parks, and beautiful nature preserves. King County Parks manages several large parcels here including some of the county's wildest Puget Sound shoreline. And the nonprofit Vashon-Maury Island Land Trust owns and manages a slew of environmentally important properties on the island graced with excellent trail networks.

Blake Island contains 5 miles of spectacular shoreline and 8 miles of trails on 475 acres. Thank Washington State Parks for that and for preserving this beautiful and intriguing island in Puget Sound. Blake Island is part of Kitsap County, but many visitors come via tour boats and private pleasure craft from Seattle marinas.

The island has a long and storied history, including claims that it was the birthplace of Chief Seattle, the Suquamish and Duwamish chief whom early Seattle settler Doc Maynard named the new city after. The island was a camping ground for the Suquamish Tribe. It's been logged and used for smuggling bootleg alcohol. It was owned and used as a private estate by a prominent Seattle millionaire for many years before becoming a Camp Fire Girls camp. It's been a state park since 1959. In 1993 President Bill Clinton held an APEC Leaders' Meeting at the park's lodge.

26   Shinglemill Creek Preserve

DISTANCE:	3 miles roundtrip
ELEVATION GAIN:	500 feet
HIGH POINT:	400 feet
DIFFICULTY:	Difficult
FITNESS:	Hikers
FAMILY-FRIENDLY:	Steep drops-offs; watch young kids
DOG-FRIENDLY:	On leash
AMENITIES:	Benches
CONTACT/MAP:	King County Parks and Vashon-Maury Island Land Trust; map available online
GPS:	N47 28.003 W122 27.924

GETTING THERE

Driving: From Seattle, take the ferry from Fauntleroy (West Seattle) to Vashon Island. Drive south on Vashon Highway SW for 3.4 miles. Turn right onto SW 156th Street and drive 0.2 mile west before turning right onto a dirt access road for Shinglemill Creek Preserve. Reach the trailhead and parking in 0.1 mile.

  Transit: King County Metro routes 118 and 119 to SW 156th Street

Follow a near-pristine creek into a deep and rugged ravine. Negotiate steep steps and traverse steep slopes as you explore Vashon's grand gulch. Pass by stumps of long-fallen giants and a few remnant old trees that escaped the axe. Then emerge at a large stream delta on secluded Fern Cove. Savor sweet views up Colvos Passage and watch for eagles, waterfowl, and salmon in this protected estuary.

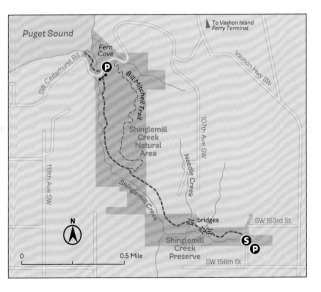

GET MOVING

The Shinglemill Creek Trail is one of the most challenging trails on the island. Requiring some real climbing and a little clambering in and out of a side gully, the trail will give you a good workout if you do this hike out and back. If the elevation gain is too much, you can always leave a car near the trail's western end on SW Cedarhurst Road and do it one-way, taking advantage of a mostly downhill trip. If you do it as a round-trip, start at the trail's eastern end as described here. Yes, it'll require a climb on the return, but it makes the hike climactic to follow the creek to the Sound. And if you want to burn more calories, there's a brand-new trail in the preserve that allows for a variation on the return.

The trail passes through properties preserved by King County Parks, the Vashon-Maury Island Land Trust, and private landowners via an easement (please stay on the trail). The preserve protects a large part of Shinglemill Creek, Vashon's second-largest creek. The creek begins at Fisher Pond, which is also protected by a land-trust preserve and is graced with trails (Trail 27).

Starting at the edge of a meadow, follow the trail west. Hop over a small creek, skirt an old orchard, and then prepare to plunge. Teetering along the crest of a forested rib, the trail drops steeply and rapidly into a ravine. Steps provide good footing and a few big trees provide stabilization. Look across the ravine to the various small slides. Don't worry, as you're on pretty solid ground on the rib.

The trail reaches the ravine bottom and crosses a side creek on a sturdy bridge. It then climbs a little and traverses a steep slope. Soon afterward the way drops steeply again. Cross Needle Creek on a good bridge and then head up again. Climb steeply via tight switchbacks and steps to a bench in the ravine high above Shinglemill Creek. Then enjoy fairly easy walking as the trail gently descends. Pass a gigantic cottonwood and at 0.9 mile come to a junction. The path

Shinglemill Creek at Fern Cove

to the right (see "Go Farther") is the Bill Mitchell Trail, opened in 2016. You want to continue left.

The trail eventually follows an old skid road, passing stumps that once supported monstrous cedars and firs. Eventually reach the ravine's bottom and follow alongside the tumbling creek beneath a mossy, verdant canopy. At 1.3 miles reach SW Cedarhurst Road (parking for a few vehicles). Cross the road and follow a boardwalk. Then cross over the creek and continue along the creek bottom (prone to flooding)—passing an old truck that must have missed the turn above—coming to Fern Cove at 1.5 miles. Here Shinglemill Creek forms a small delta feeding into Colvos Passage. When the tide is low, explore the flats. Anytime, enjoy the view out to the Kitsap Peninsula and Blake Island. Watch for salmon and eagles. Rest up for the climb back.

GO FARTHER

From the SW Cedarhurst Road Trailhead, carefully walk north along the road a few hundred feet (and climbing almost 100 feet) to the Bill Mitchell Trail (named for a late Vashon-Maury Island Land Trust member who donated the easement for the main trail) on your right. Then follow this twisting path through mature forest, climbing more than 200 feet. The trail then drops more than 100 feet to connect with the main trail at 1.2 miles. From here, head left 0.9 mile back to your start.

27 | Fisher Pond Preserve

DISTANCE:	3.2 miles of trails
ELEVATION GAIN:	Up to 300 feet
HIGH POINT:	450 feet
DIFFICULTY:	Easy to moderate
FITNESS:	Hikers, runners
FAMILY-FRIENDLY:	Yes
DOG-FRIENDLY:	On leash in Agren Park; prohibited in Fisher Pond Preserve
AMENITIES:	Benches, privy
CONTACT/MAP:	Vashon Park District and Vashon-Maury Island Land Trust; map available online from land trust
GPS:	N47 26.927 W122 30.035

GETTING THERE

Driving: From Seattle, take the ferry from Fauntleroy (West Seattle) to Vashon Island. Then drive south on Vashon Highway SW for 4.6 miles to Vashon center. At the four-way stop, turn right onto SW Bank Road and drive 1.8 miles. Turn right into Agren Memorial Park and proceed 0.1 mile to parking and trailhead.

Alternative starts can be found 0.3 mile east of Agren Memorial Park on SW Bank Road at the Vashon Park District

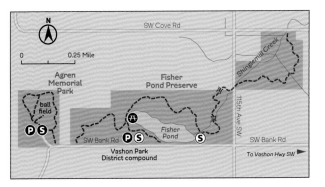

compound (parking) and 0.8 mile east on SW Bank Road near the east end of Fisher Pond (limited parking).

Hike through mature forest and thickets of evergreen huckleberries to the tranquil shoreline of Vashon's largest pond. Take time to scan the pond's placid waters for avian life, as this is one of the best places on the island for birding. It's a great place for an extended hike or trail run too, since trails extend beyond the pond both east and west.

GET MOVING

Long known as Frenchmans Pond, this large body of water was renamed Fisher Pond to honor the man responsible for its preservation. In 1998 Bill Fisher gave to the Vashon-Maury Island Land Trust 90 acres containing the pond and prime forestland. It was (and still is) the trust's largest individual donation. Subsequent land acquisition has increased the preserve to 150 acres.

Add nearby 30-acre Agren Memorial Park to the mix and you have an even larger greenbelt.

You can hike, walk, or run the trails along (but not completely around) the pond, or better yet start in Agren Memorial Park (as suggested here) and head out for longer adventures to and past the pond. Agren Memorial Park honors Lieutenant Harold E. Agren who died in a prisoner of war camp in World War II. His family donated the property in 1956 to serve as a memorial and a park. Here a half-mile trail and a short side trail circle through tall timber surrounding a ball field. Check them out and then continue on a short trail southeast of the ball field that leads to Bank Road.

Now walk east a short distance on the sometimes grassy, sometimes dusty road shoulder to the signed Fisher Pond Trailhead. Note that this trail and the preserve are closed to dogs, honoring Bill's desire that the area remain a haven for wildlife. Please adhere to this request. Nearby Island Center Forest (Trail 28) contains miles of dog-friendly trails.

The trail enters forest with a thick understory of tall evergreen huckleberry bushes. After a short descent it crosses a private road and soon reaches a junction. The way left heads to private property, so go right and quickly come to another junction. The route to the right leads to a Vashon Park District compound and an alternative trailhead—and to a trail that hugs the southern shore of Fisher Pond for about 0.25 mile. It offers some good views of the peaceful pond.

The main trail—now an old road—heads left, soon coming to a picnic shelter with a great pond view. The path continues east, veering away from the pond and eventually coming to a junction. The trail to the right leads a short way to an alternative trailhead on Bank Road. From this point directly back to Agren Memorial Park is about one mile. If you want to hike more, take the trail veering left. This lightly used path parallels Fisher's outlet creek, which forms the headwaters of Shinglemill Creek.

After passing an old orchard and scrappy forest, the trail reenters attractive forest. It crosses the creek twice—one crossing unbridged. At about 0.4 mile it crosses 115th Avenue SW, and then continues along the creek. It then climbs a little, skirting old pasture and dropping into and climbing out

Placid Fisher Pond

of some old quarries since reclaimed by the forest. At 1 mile it terminates at SW Cove Road. This is a quiet stretch of trail that can get a little muddy during wet periods. If you hike all the trails out and back within the Fisher Pond Preserve and Agren Memorial Park, you'll tally over 6 miles.

28   Island Center Forest

DISTANCE:	More than 10 miles of trails
ELEVATION GAIN:	Up to 200 feet
HIGH POINT:	425 feet
DIFFICULTY:	Easy to moderate
FITNESS:	Hikers, runners
FAMILY-FRIENDLY:	Yes, but trails are also open to mountain bikes and horses
DOG-FRIENDLY:	On leash
AMENITIES:	Privies, map kiosks, benches, picnic shelter, interpretive signs
CONTACT/MAP:	King County Parks and Vashon-Maury Island Land Trust; map available online
GPS:	N47 26.279 W122 28.240

GETTING THERE

Driving: From Seattle, take the ferry from Fauntleroy (West Seattle) to Vashon Island. Then drive south on Vashon Highway SW 5.1 miles (passing through Vashon center). Turn right onto SW 188th Street and proceed for 0.3 mile. Then turn right onto 107th Avenue SW and continue 0.1 mile to trailhead and parking.

Additional parking and an alternative trailhead can be found at the Cemetery Trailhead. Continue south on Vashon Highway SW for another 0.5 mile. Then turn left on SW Cemetery Road and drive west 1 mile. Turn right onto dirt 115th Avenue SW and reach the trailhead in 0.2 mile.

Transit: King County Metro routes 118 and 119 service Vashon Highway SW. Stop at SW 188th Street and walk west for 0.3 mile. Then turn right onto 107th Avenue SW and walk 0.1 mile to trailhead.

As the name denotes, this forested preserve sits in the center of Vashon Island. At 440 acres, the Island Center Forest is

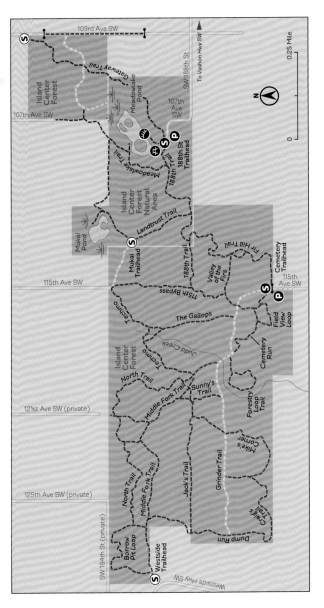

Island Center Forest
103rd Ave SW
SW 188th St
To Vashon Hwy SW
0.25 Mile
0
N
Gateway Trail
Island Center Forest
107th Ave SW
Meadowlake Pond
107th Ave SW
Meadowlake Trail
188th St Trailhead
188th Trail
Island Center Forest Natural Area
Landtrust Trail
Mukai Pond
Mukai Trailhead
188th Trail
Fir Hill Trail
Valley of the Firs
Cemetery Trailhead
115th Ave SW
115th Bypass
Techmo
115th Ave SW
Field View Loop
The Gallops
Judd Creek
Techmo
Cemetery Run
Island Center Forest
North Trail
Middle Fork Trail
Sunny's Trail
Forestry Loop Trail
121st Ave SW (private)
Mike's Corner
Grinder Trail
Jack's Trail
North Trail
Middle Fork Trail
125th Ave SW (private)
Craig's Trail
Dump Run
SW 184th St (private)
Borrow Pit Loop
Westside Trailhead
Westside Hwy SW

Meadowlake Pond

the largest parcel of public land on the island. And containing more than 10 miles of interconnected trails, it is one of the best places on Vashon for an all-day hike or a long trail run. Island Center is graced with tracts of mature timber, two large bodies of water, and the headwaters of Judd Creek. The terrain is level to rolling, making it perfect for hikers and runners of all fitness levels.

GET MOVING

A former Washington DNR property, the Island Center Forest was secured by King County Parks in 2005, and the Vashon-Maury Island Land Trust made subsequent purchases of adjoining tracts. Once used primarily for timber production, the forest is now managed for sustainable forestry, passive recreation, and wildlife habitat. And while parts of it were clear-cut in the past, there are several attractive stands of mature second-growth timber within this forest.

There are several trailheads providing access into this sprawling forest, with the Cemetery and 188th Street trailheads offering the most parking. The 188th Street Trailhead, complete with privies and a picnic shelter, is the most popular access point. The Cemetery Trailhead is more centrally located, allowing for more loop options. Strong hikers and runners can sample all or nearly all of the forest's trails within a day; most hikers and runners will assemble shorter loops. The online map is an excellent and accurate resource.

The forest is shared by horseback riders and mountain bikers. Some of the trails are more flowy, favoring bikers, but they make excellent hiking and running trails as well. Following are a few suggested routes.

Meadowlake Pond Loop: From the 188th Street Trailhead, take the short spur from the picnic area to an observation platform overlooking the forest's largest body of water. Then hike or run around it by taking the 188th Trail to the Meadowlake Trail to an old woods road to the Gateway Trail returning to your start in 1.1 miles.

Mukai Pond–Meadowlake Pond Loop: From the 188th Street Trailhead, follow the 188th Trail to the Landtrust Trail. Soon reach the Mukai Trailhead (also reached via a narrow dirt road). Now walk the Mukai Meadow Trail along Mukai Pond, which is named for the Japanese American family that once ran a successful strawberry farming operation here. The area has since reverted to a wild state supporting an abundance of birds. Note that this trail is prone to flooding in the winter. Continue on this trail to the Meadowlake Trail and then head left for a 1.5-mile loop, or right for a 1.2-mile loop.

Middle Fork–North Trail Loop: From the Cemetery Trailhead, take the Grinder (old road) Trail to the Middle Fork Trail, (reached just after crossing Judd Creek). Then follow this wooded route to the Borrow Pit Loop. Make the loop around the old quarry and return via the North Trail back to the Middle Fork and Grinder trails. Reach your start in 2.8 miles.

Forestry Loop Trail: This is a beautiful little interpretive trail through stately cedars. Reach it via the Grinder Trail from the Cemetery Trailhead. The trip is an easy 0.8 mile.

Island Center Forest Periphery: With your map in hand, tie together a series of trails along the park's periphery for a trip of around 5.5 to 6 miles.

29 Judd Creek Loop Trail

DISTANCE:	1 mile roundtrip
ELEVATION GAIN:	80 feet
HIGH POINT:	170 feet
DIFFICULTY:	Easy
FITNESS:	Hikers
FAMILY-FRIENDLY:	Yes
DOG-FRIENDLY:	On leash
AMENITIES:	None
CONTACT/MAP:	Vashon-Maury Island Land Trust; no map available online
GPS:	N47 24.947 W122 28.573

GETTING THERE

Driving: From Seattle, take the ferry from Fauntleroy (West Seattle) to Vashon Island. Then drive 6.5 miles south on Vashon Highway SW (passing through Vashon center). Turn right onto SW 204th Street and drive 0.7 mile. Then turn left onto 111th Avenue SW and continue 0.4 mile to the trailhead and roadside parking on your left.

From Tacoma, take the ferry from Point Defiance to the Tahlequah Ferry Terminal. Then drive north on Vashon Highway SW for 6.4 miles. Turn left onto SW 216th Street and drive 0.8 mile, bearing right onto 111th Avenue SW. Continue 0.2 mile north to trailhead and roadside parking on your right.

Bridge over Judd Creek

Walk along a salmon-rearing creek and through open pasture rife with birds in an area named Paradise Valley by early homesteaders. This delightful loop trail travels through the Judd Creek Preserve. It's one of the Vashon-Maury Island Land Trust's newest preserves—protecting land once part of the second-oldest homestead on the island. The trail is easy, ideal for all ages, and perfect for introducing newbies to hiking and nature.

GET MOVING

The trail enters forest and immediately comes to a junction. It's a loop so either way will do. If you opt to go right, you'll walk along Judd Creek, one of two creeks on Vashon Island that bear salmon. Judd Creek is also the island's longest creek, starting from Fisher Pond and flowing south into Quartermaster Harbor.

In spring the creek's floodplain sprouts clumps of pungent skunk cabbage. The surrounding forest has long been logged, but mature trees stand here and there, including a pair of hemlocks growing from a big cedar stump. Land Trust volunteers and others have been busy ridding the property of invasive plants and replacing them with native flora.

The trail crosses a couple of boardwalks and eventually bends east to cross the creek on a good bridge. The way then skirts an active farm and turns north, meandering through an old pasture. It returns to forest once again before passing

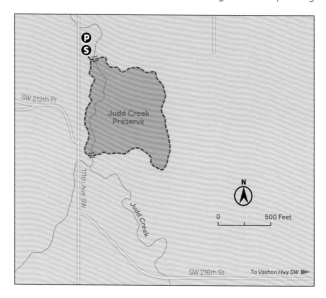

through another pasture. The trail then meets up with Judd Creek again and crosses it on another sturdy bridge just before reaching the junction near the trailhead.

GO FARTHER

Nearby are a couple of other small Vashon-Maury Island Land Trust properties with family-friendly trails. Check out the 0.7-mile trail that loops around forested Christensen Pond (off of Wax Orchard Road SW just south of SW 232nd Street). And at the Land Trust's newest property, Frog Holler Forest (off of Wax Orchard Road SW, 0.5 mile south of the Bates Walk SW junction), you can hike on 2 miles of trail traversing this 60-acre property.

30 Burton Acres Park

DISTANCE:	More than 1.5 miles of trails
ELEVATION GAIN:	Up to 140 feet
HIGH POINT:	140 feet
DIFFICULTY:	Easy
FITNESS:	Hikers, walkers, runners
FAMILY-FRIENDLY:	Yes
DOG-FRIENDLY:	On leash
AMENITIES:	Privy and picnic tables at Jensen Point
CONTACT/MAP:	Vashon Park District; no map available online
GPS:	N47 23.387 W122 26.936

GETTING THERE

Driving: From Seattle, take the ferry from Fauntleroy (West Seattle) to Vashon Island. Then drive 8.9 miles south on Vashon Highway SW (passing through Vashon center) to the hamlet of Burton. Turn left onto SW Burton Drive and continue for 0.4 mile. Then turn right onto SW Bayview Drive (which becomes SW Harbor Drive) and proceed 0.8 mile. Turn right into Jensen Point Park and parking.

From Tacoma, take the ferry from Point Defiance to the Tahlequah Ferry Terminal. Then drive north on Vashon Highway SW for 4.9 miles to the hamlet of Burton. Turn right onto SW Burton Drive and follow the preceding directions.

Transit: King County Metro Route 118 services Burton. From there walk west 0.5 mile on quiet SW Burton Drive to the park's east exit (Ames Road Trailhead).

Situated on the Burton Peninsula a hop, skip, and jump from the historic community of Burton, Burton Acres Park has an almost New England feeling to it. The park is small, but trails meander all through the stately second growth gracing this park. It's easy to get disoriented on the mostly unmarked trails, but you really can't get lost here, so enjoy walking or running willy-nilly through the forest.

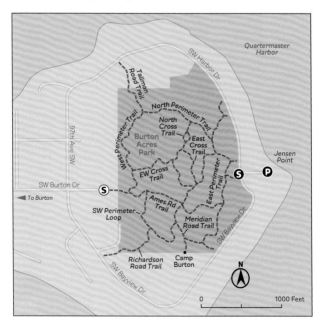

Towering firs at Burton Acres Park

GET MOVING

Located just a few minutes from the quaint village of Burton, this park and its environs harken back to a quieter, slower past. The area teems with history. It was the home to one of the first colleges in the state, Vashon College, which operated from 1892 to 1912. None of its buildings remain.

From Jensen Point Park check out the beach on Quartermaster Harbor and then walk across SW Harbor Drive to the trailhead. You quickly come to a trail sign, but don't be deceived, as almost all the junctions in this 64-acre park are unmarked. The trails are all named, however—you just won't know which one you are on! You will almost assuredly get lost. But don't despair, as the park is small. If you end up at one of the many secondary trailheads or adjacent Camp Burton, just retreat.

The terrain is heavily forested, and the peninsula harboring the park is a little hilly too, so you can get some vertical in as you circle around a couple of times. There are trails that run the perimeter of the park, and if you follow them without deviating onto side trails you'll cover around a mile. You can easily walk or run a few miles by doing all the interior trails and doubling back. There are a couple of benches among the timber if you need to sit down and get oriented. Have fun!

31 Dockton Forest and Maury Island Natural Area

DISTANCE:	More than 10 miles of trails
ELEVATION GAIN:	Up to 450 feet
HIGH POINT:	375 feet
DIFFICULTY:	Easy to moderate
FITNESS:	Hikers, runners
FAMILY-FRIENDLY:	Yes, but some trails see heavy mountain bike use
DOG-FRIENDLY:	On leash
AMENITIES:	Privies, map kiosks
CONTACT/MAP:	King County Parks; map available online
GPS:	N47 22.194 W122 27.242

GETTING THERE

Driving: From Seattle, take the ferry from Fauntleroy (West Seattle) to Vashon Island. Then drive 6.5 miles south on Vashon Highway SW (passing through Vashon center). Turn left onto SW 204th Street and drive 0.4 mile. Bear left onto SW Ellisport Road and continue 0.7 mile. Turn right onto George Edwards Road (Dockton Road SW). Follow this road onto Maury Island, coming to Dockton Park at 4.4 miles. Trailhead and parking are on the left.

From Tacoma, take the ferry from Point Defiance to the Tahlequah Ferry Terminal. Then drive north on Vashon Highway SW for 5.8 miles. Turn right onto SW Quartermaster Drive and drive 1.4 miles to Maury Island. Bear right onto George

Deserted beach in the Maury Island Natural Area

Edwards Road (Dockton Road SW) and continue for 3.5 miles to Dockton Park.

Transit: King County Metro Route 119

A wild coastline abutting an abandoned gravel quarry surrounded by stands of tall timber, the Dockton Forest and adjoining Maury Island Natural Area comprise 426 acres. One of the largest tracts of public land on the island, the area contains more than 10 miles (and counting) of multiuse trails to explore. Popular with mountain bikers, these parks are also admired by hikers and trail runners. Walk a deserted beach, climb towering bluffs, run through attractive stands of forest, and get in a great workout.

GET MOVING

The Maury Island Natural Area was once owned by a gravel-mining consortium. In the late 1990s the owners proposed a mining operation that would have quarried up to 7.5 million tons of gravel a year. This excavation would have required building a massive dock for loading huge barges around the clock. The operation would have destroyed eelgrass beds and some of the largest stands of madronas in the state, and threatened water supplies with arsenic contamination. After a long battle spearheaded by the citizens group Preserve our Islands and other conservation groups, the mine was stopped. In the last days of 2010, the 235-acre quarry property became a King County park.

From the Dockton Park Trailhead you can set out—and up—on a series of trails and old woods roads through a forest of Douglas fir and madronas. The trails are unmarked and navigation can be confusing. The easiest option is to stick with the trail heading east and paralleling SW 260th Street. This trail was recently rebuilt by the Vashon Mountain Bike Association and is popular with bikes. In 0.4 mile you'll come upon a trailhead on SW 260th Street (alternative start). Here a newly emerging mountain bike trail network radiates south.

The best option for runners and hikers is to continue east another 0.1 mile, reaching a gated gravel road. This is the old quarry access road. Turn right and hike it (passing an old road-trail on your left), coming to a junction in 0.2 mile. Here you have some options. You can continue on the old road, winding down 300 feet into the quarry, passing rusting conveyors and other old excavating machinery, and reaching the old dock site and beach access in 0.8 mile.

The trail right (west) leads to the mountain bike trail network. The trail left—an old road—is a great option. Follow this path, which winds along the rim of the old quarry, to excellent bluff-top viewpoints. Here gaze across the dormant rock pit to Puget Sound. Enjoy views that include South Sound cities,

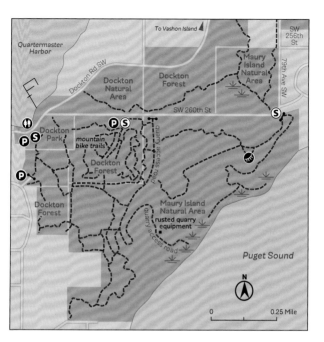

the Issaquah Alps, and Mount Rainier. At 0.5 mile this trail comes to a junction. The way left leads back to the quarry access road. The way right swings around to another excellent viewpoint. The main trail continues straight, passing an area recently scrubbed for arsenic (from fallout from the now-closed and decommissioned Asarco smelter in Tacoma) and replanted. At 0.8 mile the trail reaches a gate at SW 260th Street (no parking).

There are some primitive trails across the street. A better option is to take the trail right from the gate. This is another old road, now cloaked in invasive and ugly Scotch broom. It descends the bluff, traversing steep old quarry slopes. In 0.5 mile it splits. Both directions go to the shore. The way left is the quicker option, delivering you to the beach in 0.1 mile.

When the tides are favorable, enjoy some great coastal walking—usually all alone on the 1-mile-long cobbled beach. Walk along the base of steep forested slopes and try to imagine how this coastline—one of the longest undeveloped stretches in King County—would have been compromised by the mining operation. When you are ready to leave the beach, take the old gravel quarry access road back. It can be picked up along the beach, 0.35 mile west of where you reached the shore if you took the quicker, 0.1-mile spur trail.

If you're looking for more trails to explore, that can be arranged. About midway on the old quarry access road at a hairpin curve, several trails depart south and west. These trails loop through forest high on the bluff, cradling the old quarry to the east. You can easily get disoriented here, so bring along your GPS and practice your navigational skills.

32 Maury Island Marine Park

DISTANCE:	3 miles of trails
ELEVATION GAIN:	Up to 475 feet
HIGH POINT:	475 feet
DIFFICULTY:	Easy to moderate
FITNESS:	Hikers, walkers, runners
FAMILY-FRIENDLY:	Yes
DOG-FRIENDLY:	On leash
AMENITIES:	Privies, map kiosks, benches, picnic shelter, interpretive signs
CONTACT/MAP:	King County Parks; map available online
GPS:	N47 23.120 W122 23.965

GETTING THERE

Driving: From Seattle, take the ferry from Fauntleroy (West Seattle) to Vashon Island. Then drive 6.5 miles south on

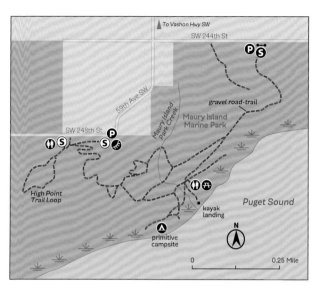

Vashon Highway SW (passing through Vashon center). Turn left onto SW 204th Street and drive 0.4 mile. Bear right onto SW Ellisport Road and continue 0.7 mile. Turn right on George Edwards Road (Dockton Road SW). Follow this road for 1.5 miles onto Maury Island and bear left onto SW Point Robinson Road. Then drive 1.4 miles and turn right onto (unsigned) 59th Avenue SW. Continue 0.3 mile and turn left onto SW 244th Street. Reach parking and the trailhead in 0.3 mile.

From Tacoma, take the ferry from Point Defiance to Tahlequah Ferry Terminal. Then drive north on Vashon Highway SW for 5.8 miles. Turn right onto SW Quartermaster Drive and drive 1.4 miles. Bear right onto George Edwards Road (Dockton Road SW) and continue 0.6 mile, bearing left onto SW Point Robinson Road. Then follow the preceding directions.

Follow an old dirt road down a forested ravine to a grassy little bench above a gorgeous strand of deserted beach. Walk the beach—then take to the park's upland trails, climbing a high grassy bluff once serving as a gravel quarry. Stop frequently to take in sweeping views of mountains and sound. The Maury Island Marine Park contains 320 wild, uncrowded acres of pure bliss.

GET MOVING

Like its neighbor, the Maury Island Natural Area, the Maury Island Marine Park was also once used for gravel mining. But the operations here ceased much longer ago, meaning Mother Nature (with a little help from human volunteers) is much further along in its restoration. And like its neighbor to the southwest, this park also contains some of the healthiest and largest stands of madronas in Puget Sound and a wild, undeveloped beach—this one 1.3 miles long. But the Marine Park, unlike the Natural Area, is much quieter, making it the better choice for getting away from it all.

The trailhead sits at an elevation of 375 feet, meaning you'll need to hike uphill on the return from the beach. That and the 0.6-mile distance of the road-trail to the beach deters casual visitors—but not you. Walk the gated road-trail down a lush ravine, then across steep slopes. At 0.4 mile reach a junction. The road continues left 0.2 mile to a picnic shelter, marine camps for paddlers, a handful of short trails, and beach access. Here a small coastal plain harbors wetlands along the shore. The public beach is more than 1.25 miles long and is secluded, seated at the base of high bluffs and ringed with big trees. The small Gold Beach Community sits between Maury Island Marine Park and Maury Island Natural Area. Otherwise, this is one long stretch of fairly wild beach.

At the aforementioned junction, a road-trail leads right crossing Maury Island Park Creek to a high grassy bench, which was once a gravel quarry. An old water tower and a few other relics still stand. There are several small trails looping around on the bench, with one leading down to the picnic

Maury Island Marine Park's inviting beach

shelter near the beach. Keep working your way west and follow a trail that climbs steeply out of the old quarry. It switchbacks on the terraced landscape, and at 0.75 mile from the
road-trail junction it comes to another junction high on the
bluff edge.

Here first head right 0.12 mile to an overlook complete
with interpretive and historical panels about this property.

The views of the South Sound, Tacoma, Mount Rainier, and the wild shoreline below are spectacular. The overlook sits near a parking area on SW 248th Street (alternative start).

Return to the bluff-rim junction, and this time head west, soon coming to another junction. Right leads a short way to a trailhead (and privy) on SW 248th Street (alternative start). Left leads to the 0.4-mile High Point Trail Loop. This path travels through meadow and forest upon the 475-foot bluff-top high point. Take in views west of the Olympic Mountains and admire exceptional madrona trees along the way.

GO FARTHER

After your hike or run at Maury Island Marine Park, make the short drive to Point Robinson Park at the end of SW Point Robinson Road. Here you'll find some short trails taking you to a sandy beach and the 1915-built lighthouse—a Vashon Island icon.

33 Blake Island Marine State Park

DISTANCE:	8 miles of trails
ELEVATION GAIN:	Up to 220 feet
HIGH POINT:	220 feet
DIFFICULTY:	Easy to moderate
FITNESS:	Hikers, runners
FAMILY-FRIENDLY:	Yes
DOG-FRIENDLY:	On leash
AMENITIES:	Restrooms, water, picnic tables, campground, interpretive signs, dock, longhouse, and café (summer only)
CONTACT/MAP:	Washington State Parks
GPS:	N47 32.531 W122 28.964
BEFORE YOU GO:	Moorage and docking fees required

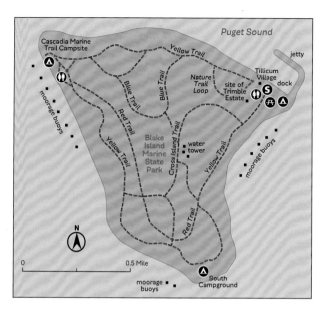

GETTING THERE:

There are no roads or ferries to Blake Island. You will need to provide your own transportation in the form of a boat or kayak. Argosy Cruises services the island as part of their Tillicum Excursion (a meal and performance at a Native American longhouse) from Seattle's Pier 54 and Bremerton (foot ferry dock). They offer some sailings with an extra hour to explore the island. Check their website for details.

A former estate, now a nearly undeveloped 475-acre island a mere 6.8 nautical miles (7.8 miles) from downtown Seattle, Blake Island is one of the star natural attractions of Puget Sound. Although it is popular with paddlers and boaters who crowd the park's docks, mooring sites, and campgrounds, landlubbers will be pleasantly surprised to find that it contains 8 miles of excellent trails. And while most human visitors stick to the island's gorgeous beaches, its trails are usually traipsed only by its large resident deer herd.

GET MOVING

From the park's busy dock, folks are usually heading left to claim a campsite, or right to Tillicum Village for a Native American dance performance and cuisine. Trails lead left and right, and as you head out on them, you soon find that the island takes on a more peaceful persona than at the dock.

Blake Island was once the personal estate of William Pitt Trimble. A lawyer from Kentucky, Trimble moved to Seattle in 1890, became involved in real estate, and by 1920 was one of the city's wealthiest residents. A series of misfortunes, however, would later lead to Trimble abandoning the island. In 1959 Blake Island became a Washington State Park.

Most of the park's trails are old service roads, making for leisurely hiking and gentle trail running. They lead around the periphery of the island to magnificent beaches and across the quiet interior. Blake is thickly forested with impressive specimens of madrona, but the understory is fairly open due to the browsing of the island's copious deer. Views from the shoreline range from the Olympic Mountains to the west, Mount Baker and Glacier Peak to the northeast, Mount Rainier to the south, and the Seattle skyline to the east. If you spend the night on the island, you'll witness a spectacular sight, Seattle's shimmering cityscape lighting the darkness.

If you only have time for a short hike, consider the 0.5-mile Nature Trail Loop, located to the west of Tillicum Village. If you've got more time, definitely hike the Yellow Trail, which circumnavigates the island for a 3.8-mile loop. Going counterclockwise you'll reach the island's best beaches at 1.2 miles. During low tides you can walk on a sandy beach and extensive tidal flats. There are campsites and restrooms here too. The trail then heads southeast to the South Campground, where there are breathtaking views of Mount Rainier and Vashon

Hiker surveying Blake Island's extensive beaches

Island. When the trail turns northeast, it follows a more hilly route, passing group campsites and the remains of the Trimble Estate.

The Blue, Red, and Cross Island trails all traverse the island's interior and offer quiet ambling, as they are lightly traveled. They don't receive as much maintenance as the Yellow Trail, so be aware of creeping nettles lest you get zapped. They're all around a mile in length and both the Blue and Cross Island trails have forking spurs. They all gain and lose a little elevation too, with the Red and Cross Island trails going over the island's 220-foot high point.

The Blue Trail passes by some wetlands, which are usually pretty dry by late summer. The island overall is a fairly dry place. Along the Blue Trail you'll pass through some cedar and grand fir groves. There are even a couple of Sitka spruces here and there. And throughout the entire island you're sure to hear and see a handful of bald eagles.

Next page: *Lush, green views along the Green River Trail (Trail 39)*

SOUTH KING COUNTY

At first glance the suburbs and cities immediately to the south of Seattle appear to offer little in the order of trails. But beyond the housing complexes, warehouses, retail outlets, manufacturing centers, and busy airport are several large parks, greenbelts, and trail networks. Venture to the communities of Burien, Tukwila, SeaTac, Des Moines, Kent, and Renton—particularly the latter two, Washington's sixth- and eighth-largest cities respectively—and find lots of trail surprises.

In these communities hike, walk, or run on trails along beautiful Puget Sound and Lake Washington shorelines. Follow trails along large rivers, through extensive wetlands, and around ponds and lakes. Take to trails traversing historic farms, settlements, and communities that rival Seattle when it comes to ethnic and cultural diversity. And let loose on some of the region's best and longest rail trails. And best of all, trails in these communities are almost always a lot less crowded than ones in Seattle.

34 Seahurst Park

DISTANCE:	About 2.5 miles of trails
ELEVATION GAIN:	400 feet
HIGH POINT:	400 feet
DIFFICULTY:	Easy to moderate
FITNESS:	Walkers, runners, hikers
FAMILY-FRIENDLY:	Yes, and some trails are paved and are wheelchair and jogger-stroller friendly
DOG-FRIENDLY:	On leash
AMENITIES:	Restrooms, picnic tables and shelters, playground, Environmental Science Center
CONTACT/MAP:	Burien Parks and Recreation
GPS:	N47 28.686 W 122 21.775
BEFORE YOU GO:	Park is open from 8:00 AM to dusk

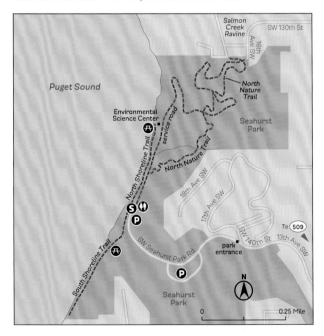

GETTING THERE

Driving: From Seattle, follow SR 99 south to the 1st Avenue S. Bridge. Continue straight on SR 509 for 4.7 miles, then take the exit for SW 146th Street (just before the exit for SR 518). Continue west on SW 146th Street for 0.7 mile. Then turn right onto Ambaum Boulevard SW and after 0.1 mile turn left onto SW 144th Street. Continue 0.2 mile and turn right onto 13th Avenue SW. Continue on this road, which becomes SW 140th Street and then SW Seahurst Park Road for 0.9 mile to the park and parking.

From Renton, follow SR 518 west, exiting onto SW 148th Street at the junction with SR 509. Then drive 0.7 mile west on SW 148th Street. Turn right onto Ambaum Boulevard SW and after 0.2 mile turn left onto SW 144th Street and follow the preceding directions.

A superb stretch of Puget Sound shoreline and a couple of miles of trails heading into ravines and up lofty forested bluffs make Seahurst Park a walker's delight. Roam on a sandy beach, admiring the Olympic Mountains across the Sound. And burn some calories taking to forested trails climbing high above the surf. Seahurst Park is one of the prettiest places between Seattle and Tacoma.

GET MOVING

A former King County Park, 182-acre Seahurst (formerly named Ed Munro Seahurst Park for the King County Commissioner responsible for its inception) is now the pride and joy of the Burien parks system. On sunny summer days the park can be packed, relegating your start to the upper parking lot. That just means you get a little more exercise walking to and from the park's trails.

From the lower lot, a paved, accessible-to-all 0.3-mile trail crosses a creek before running south along the shoreline. A paved trail also leads north along the shore, traveling

Hiker enjoying Seahurst Park's beach

0.3 mile to the Environmental Science Center (check out http://envsciencecenter.org for its programs), a Marine Tech Lab, and picnic areas. If the tide is low, consider walking the fine beach. Until recently, the shore here was marred by a bulkhead. Park personnel and volunteers have done a wonderful job restoring the shore to a more natural state. Seahurst's shore is a great place for birding too—look for harlequin ducks—particularly in the winter months.

If you're looking for a workout, take to the park's dirt service road (which serves as a wide trail) and the North Nature Trail. The service road starts right by the restrooms near the lower parking lot. Follow it north for an easy start as it parallels the North Shoreline Trail. It then starts to climb and makes a long switchback. Next, it traverses steep wooded slopes above a ravine before winding its way farther up the bluff. In 1 mile it terminates at 16th Avenue SW (no parking). You'll have gained 400 vertical feet along the way.

The North Nature Trail begins from the service road about 0.1 mile from the lower parking lot. This delightful path cuts through thick vegetation beneath a luxuriant forest canopy and enters a deep ravine. It then crosses a small creek before climbing more steeply out of the ravine. The trail crosses the service road thrice before terminating high on the bluff near the 16th Avenue SW park entrance. The trail climbs more than 400 vertical feet over its 0.75-mile course. Combine it with the service road for a loop, opting to return on the road for a descent that's gentler on your knees.

GO FARTHER

Walk a short distance north on 16th Avenue SW and come to a trailhead for Salmon Creek Ravine Park. There are several miles of primitive trails in this 88-acre greenbelt. You can also access this park from its main trailhead located to the left of the gated wastewater treatment plant entrance off of Shorewood Drive SW.

35 North SeaTac Park

DISTANCE:	More than 5 miles of trails
ELEVATION GAIN:	Up to 250 feet
HIGH POINT:	400 feet
DIFFICULTY:	Easy
FITNESS:	Walkers, runners
FAMILY-FRIENDLY:	Yes, and paved trails are wheelchair and jogger-stroller friendly
DOG-FRIENDLY:	On leash
AMENITIES:	Restrooms, playground, picnic shelter, sports fields, botanical garden, community center
CONTACT/MAP:	SeaTac Parks, Community Programs and Services
GPS:	N47 29.214 W122 18.490
BEFORE YOU GO:	Park is open from dawn to dusk

GETTING THERE

Driving: From Seattle, follow SR 99 south to 1st Avenue S. Bridge. Continue straight on SR 509 for 4 miles, taking the exit for S. 128th Street. Continue east on S. 128th Street for 1.1 miles. Then turn right onto 20th Avenue S. and drive 0.2 mile to the park and trailhead.

From Renton, follow I-405 to SR 518. Continue west on SR 518 (passing Sea-Tac Airport) for 2.3 miles and exit onto Des Moines Memorial Drive South. Turn right and follow this road for 1.3 miles. Then turn right onto S. 128th Street. Continue east 0.2 mile and turn right onto 20th Avenue S. Then drive 0.2 mile to the park and trailhead.

Transit: King County Metro Route 132

Run or walk on a network of paved and soft-surface forested trails in this large park just north of busy Sea-Tac Airport. Want a good workout? Run or walk the 3-mile Westside Trail from the park all the way to the airport! Consider diverting onto the adjacent Miller Creek Trail through restored wetlands, where you can watch for birds and the big Boeing and Airbus birds above.

GET MOVING

North SeaTac Park has got a lot going for it, from ball fields and courts to a BMX track and trails—lots of them. Paved paths traverse manicured lawns and circle playfields. Soft-surface trails wind through the southern wooded portions of the park. And a 3-mile paved path leaves the park, connecting to other trails for even longer wanderings.

This park is just north of Sea-Tac Airport and right below its flight path. Matter of fact, the park was created in the late 1990s as mitigation to runway expansion. The Port of Seattle purchased entire old residential blocks and commenced with developing this fine park. Being near the nation's ninth-busiest airport, however, means lots of noise—at times

deafening. You may want to consider earbuds while walking and running the paths here—especially the Westside Trail leading to the airport.

You can easily put in a few miles of running or walking here just by sticking to the near-level paths in the heart of the park. But if you want a longer workout, head out on the long Westside Trail leading south. This path passes the Sunset Park playfields and then parallels Des Moines Memorial Drive. The parkway was dedicated in 1922 and lined with 1432 elm trees to commemorate Washington's World War I dead. Some of the old trees are still standing—look for them along the way.

Ignore paths that lead left to Tub Lake, which unfortunately has become a beacon for homeless camps and drug use. City officials are aware of the situation and are addressing it. Just

Landing plane above the Miller Creek Trail

beyond S. 144th Street you'll come to the trailhead (located across the parkway) to the new Miller Creek Trail. This short paved path meanders across mitigated wetlands and is worth a look-see.

If you continue on the Westside Trail, use caution where it darts under SR 518, as drivers exiting and entering this freeway are not always attentive. The path then continues along the parkway to S. 156th Way. Here it connects with the Lake to Sound Trail—a 16-mile King County Regional Trail currently under construction (and utilizing some existing trails) spanning from the Des Moines waterfront to Lake Washington in Renton.

The Westside Trail now continues east (as part of the Lake to Sound Trail) 1.1 miles, following S. 156th Way (which becomes S. 154th Street) and starts to climb. On the left are woods and wetlands along Miller Creek. On the right—runways! Duck under landing lights and reach the trail's terminus at some businesses near the junction of S. 154th Street and 24th Avenue S. Beyond, the way follows bike paths more appealing to cyclists than pedestrians.

GO FARTHER

At the intersection of Des Moines Memorial Drive S. and S. 156th Way, you can walk or run a new (opened in 2017) section of the Lake to Sound Trail south for 1.5 miles. King County Parks hopes to soon construct the next section of this trail—a 2.2-mile continuing stretch that will connect with the Des Moines Creek Trail (Trail 36).

36 Des Moines Creek Trail

DISTANCE:	4 miles roundtrip
ELEVATION GAIN:	230 feet
HIGH POINT:	250 feet
DIFFICULTY:	Easy
FITNESS:	Walkers, runners
FAMILY-FRIENDLY:	Yes, and paved trails are wheelchair and jogger-stroller friendly
DOG-FRIENDLY:	On leash
AMENITIES:	Restrooms, picnic tables, historic structures, interpretive signs
CONTACT/MAP:	Des Moines Parks, Recreation and Senior Services (no map online)
GPS:	N47 24.367 W122 19.656
BEFORE YOU GO:	Parking is limited at trailheads; additional parking is available at nearby Des Moines Marina (fee charged)

GETTING THERE

Driving: From Seattle or Tacoma, follow I-5 to exit 149. Then follow SR 516 (Kent-Des Moines Road) west for 1.9 miles. Bear right onto SR 509 (Marine View Drive S.) and proceed for 0.3 mile. Then turn left onto S. 223rd Street and continue for 0.1 mile. Bear right onto Cliff Avenue S. and follow for 0.2 mile to Des Moines Beach Park and the trailhead.

For an alternative start from the northern trailhead, from Seattle or Tacoma, follow I-5 to exit 151. Then follow S. 200th Street west for 0.9 mile to the trailhead and parking on your left.

Transit: King County Metro routes RapidRide A, 121, and 166 stop on Marine View Drive S., from which it is a short walk on sidewalks to the park and trailhead.

One of the loveliest trails in South King County, this paved path follows a cascading creek through a twisting green ravine. Start at a historic camp on a pretty little beach and wind your way up along the waterway through a greenbelt. You'll feel like you're far from civilization until the surrounding thrush songs and water music are interrupted by jet noise— reminding you that hectic Sea-Tac Airport lies just beyond this peaceful ribbon of forest.

GET MOVING

The Des Moines Creek Trail starts from Des Moines Beach Park, a beautiful and historically significant 19.6-acre tract where Des Moines Creek empties into the Sound. The park has preserved the remnants of an old church camp—constructed from the 1920s to 1940s—that is a great representation of the scores of such fishing, resort, and church camps that once lined Puget Sound. Today very few structures from this bygone time remain.

The trail starts just to the east of the old auditorium. Immediately begin following Des Moines Creek upstream. The route darts under the tall Marine View Drive bridge and begins to slowly gain elevation. Big cottonwoods and maples line the way. Quarter-mile posts help you keep track of your distance covered. At 0.75 mile the natural surroundings are temporarily suspended as the trail skirts a wastewater treatment plant.

At 0.9 mile a short trail leads left to S. 211th Place. At 1.2 miles a much longer, soft-surface trail leads right. It crosses the creek on a sturdy bridge and then winds through forest, climbing out of the ravine. It then passes an old industrial area and terminates on S. 216th Street at about 0.5 mile.

The Des Moines Creek Trail continues winding up the ravine, paralleling the tumbling creek. After about 1.6 miles you'll notice a few dirt trails taking off left—these are popular with mountain bikers, and trail runners may find them worth checking out. The trail crosses into SeaTac and descends

Busy dog-walker on the Des Moines Creek Trail

slightly to reach its northern trailhead (alternative start; parking, no facilities) on S. 200th Street. For now this is it, but King County Parks is getting close to extending this trail by 2.2 miles to connect with the Westside Trail in North SeaTac Park (Trail 35) to become part of the new 16-mile Lake to Sound Trail. Keep returning to check on its progress.

GO FARTHER

Walk or run downstream through the historic section of Des Moines Beach Park. A paved path heads to the beach and then makes a bridged crossing of the creek to connect with the city's marina. You can add another mile by going out and back to the marina.

37 Saltwater State Park

DISTANCE:	More than 2 miles of trails
ELEVATION GAIN:	Up to 200 feet
HIGH POINT:	150 feet
DIFFICULTY:	Easy
FITNESS:	Walkers, hikers
FAMILY-FRIENDLY:	Yes
DOG-FRIENDLY:	On leash
AMENITIES:	Restrooms, picnic tables, campground, interpretive center
CONTACT/MAP:	Washington State Parks
GPS:	N47 22.434 W122 19.319
BEFORE YOU GO:	Discover Pass required; park is open from 8:00 AM to dusk

GETTING THERE

Driving: From Seattle, follow I-5 to exit 149. Then follow SR 516 (Kent–Des Moines Road) west for 1.2 miles. Turn left onto 16th Avenue S. and continue for 0.4 mile. Then turn right onto S. 240th Street and drive 0.5 mile. Next, turn left onto Marine View Drive S. and drive 0.8 mile. Turn right onto S. 252nd Street

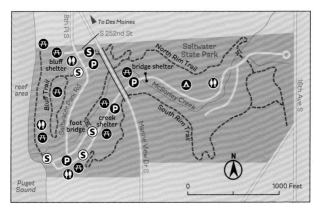

and then immediately turn left onto Saltwater Park Road and drive 0.2 mile to parking and trailhead.

From Tacoma, follow I-5 to exit 147. Turn left onto S. 272nd Street and drive 0.9 mile.Then turn right onto 16th Avenue S. and continue for 1.4 miles. Next, turn left onto S. 250th Street, which becomes S. 251st Street, and drive 0.4 mile, crossing Marine View Drive S. Then turn left onto 8th Place S., which becomes Saltwater Park Road, and drive 0.2 mile to parking and trailhead.

Transit: King County Metro Route 121 stops at the corner of S. 251st Street and Marine View Drive S.

Most (and there are many) visitors come to this state park to play or lounge along its nearly 1500 feet of undeveloped shoreline. Leave them behind and discover a quieter side of this 88-acre park by taking to its 2-plus miles of trails. Loop around a deep, forested ravine cradling a creekside campground. Duck beneath a towering bridge and saunter on small wooded bridges spanning a salmon-rearing creek.

GET MOVING

Located within the suburban sprawl between Seattle and Tacoma, this small state park is one of the most visited within the state. An enticing beach, underwater reef, large picnic area, and 47-site campground are the park's main draws. Its trails, however, are often overlooked, allowing for peaceful (except for planes flying overhead) wanderings and a glimpse of what this area once looked like before settlement reached a frenzy.

Encompassing a ravine cut by McSorley Creek and a stretch of scenic shoreline, this park also has an interesting history. It was here in 1933 that civic leaders from Seattle and Tacoma figuratively buried the hatchet to their long-running feuding by literally burying a hatchet. The new park was later developed by the Civilian Conservation Corps. Check out the

Bridge along North Rim Trail in Saltwater State Park

attractive structures displaying their fine craftsmanship after finishing your hike.

From the large parking lot, follow the Yellow Loop (consisting of both the South and North Rim trails), which travels 1.5

miles around the ravine. The southern half of this loop climbs to the ravine's rim and then traverses its steep slopes, darting in and out of side gullies. The northern half of the trail stays closer to the ravine's base, traveling a short distance alongside salmon-spawning McSorley Creek.

Along the entire loop there are some good views below and you get to pass beneath the attractive Marine View Drive bridge twice. You also get to make several bridged crossings of McSorley Creek and its tributaries. There are impressive grand firs along the trail and unfortunately patches of invasive ivy. The trail passes through the campground too. A side trail heads south to a neighborhood, and another side trail heads north to the ranger station.

Near the ranger station and small interpretive center, find the pleasant Bluff Trail (Green Loop). This interpretive trail makes a 0.3-mile loop on a bluff above the ravine at its mouth on the Sound. And definitely don't skip the 0.3-mile paved shoreline path with its excellent views of Vashon Island and the Olympic Mountains. It is exceptionally pretty when the evening light dances upon the Sound's salty waters.

38 Interurban Trail (South)

DISTANCE:	15 miles one-way
ELEVATION GAIN:	Up to 100 feet
HIGH POINT:	80 feet
DIFFICULTY:	Easy
FITNESS:	Walkers, runners
FAMILY-FRIENDLY:	Yes, and paved trail is jogger-stroller and wheelchair friendly
DOG-FRIENDLY:	On leash
AMENITIES:	Restrooms, benches
CONTACT/MAP:	King County Parks
GPS:	N47 28.118 W122 15.002

Walking a quiet section of Interurban Trail (South)

GETTING THERE

Driving to Fort Dent Park: From Seattle, follow I-5 south to exit 156. Turn left on Interurban Avenue S. and drive 1.7 miles. Then turn left onto Fort Dent Way and drive 0.1 mile. Next, turn left onto Starfire Way and continue 0.25 mile to parking and the trailhead.

From Tacoma, follow I-5 north to I-405 and take exit 1. Turn left onto Interurban Avenue S. and drive 0.3 mile. Then turn right onto Fort Dent Way and follow the preceding directions.

Driving to Foster Park: From Seattle or Tacoma, follow I-5 to exit 149. Then head east on SR 516 (Kent-Des Moines Road, which becomes Willis Street) for 3.2 miles (just beyond the SR 167 interchange). Turn right onto 74th Avenue S. (which becomes S. 259th Street) and drive 0.7 mile to the trailhead and parking.

Other Trail Access Points: Interurban Trail Park in Tukwila at Nelson Place and Longacres Way; Kent Rotary Basketball Court (near Kent/James Street Park and Ride in downtown

The Interurban continues south, paralleling the West Valley Highway and active railroad tracks. At 2.6 miles the trail passes beneath S. 180th Street. Here you can take a path right and then walk S. 180th through the old train-stop community of Orillia, reaching the Green River Trail in 0.3 mile for yet another loop option.

The Interurban continues south, passing warehouses and light industries, drainage ditches and small wetlands. It crosses beneath S. 196th Street and makes a surface crossing (use signals at all surface crossings) of S. 212th Street. Approaching downtown Kent, the trail crosses a blighted area where transients may be a concern. It then passes beneath SR 167, reaching W. James Street at about 6.4 miles. It then skirts playfields and empty city lots and crosses some busy streets. After crossing Willis Street at 7 miles, the trail leaves urban blight behind and becomes an enjoyable pathway again. At 7.6 miles the trail comes to Foster Park and once again intersects the Green River Trail, where a 19.5-mile loop can be made back to Fort Dent.

The trail again crosses the Green River and continues south alongside railroad sidings. At 8.7 miles it passes beneath S. 277th Street. At 9.5 miles it crosses 37th Street NW. The trail then traverses lush, expansive wetlands and passes the Emerald Downs Racetrack. After ducking beneath 15th Street NW, the trail crosses Auburn's W. Main Street at 11.9 miles. After crossing busy 15th Street SW at 12.8 miles, the way bends southwest.

The trail then passes through Algona, coming to Ellingson Road at 14.6 miles. This is a good spot to call it quits. But if you want to keep going, the trail continues to Pacific in Pierce County for another 0.5 mile (on a path that can use some maintenance), ending at 3rd Avenue SW.

GO FARTHER

An unconnected section of the trail continues in Milton.

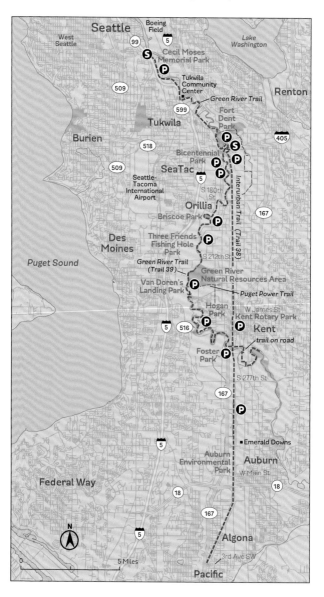

39 Green River Trail

DISTANCE:	19.6 miles one-way
ELEVATION GAIN:	Up to 50 feet
HIGH POINT:	50 feet
DIFFICULTY:	Easy
FITNESS:	Walkers, runners
FAMILY-FRIENDLY:	Yes, and paved trail is jogger-stroller and wheelchair friendly
DOG-FRIENDLY:	On leash
AMENITIES:	Restrooms, benches, playgrounds, public art
CONTACT/MAP:	King County Parks
GPS:	N47 28.118 W122 15.002

GETTING THERE

Driving to Fort Dent Park: From Seattle, follow I-5 south to exit 156. Turn left on Interurban Avenue S. and drive 1.7 miles. Then turn left onto Fort Dent Way and drive 0.1 mile. Next, turn left onto Starfire Way and continue 0.25 mile to parking and the trailhead.

From Tacoma, follow I-5 north to I-405 and take exit 1. Turn left onto Interurban Avenue S. and drive 0.3 mile. Then turn right onto Fort Dent Way and follow the preceding directions.

Driving to Hogan Park: From Seattle or Tacoma, follow I-5 to exit 149. Then head east on SR 516 (Kent-Des Moines Road) for 1.6 miles. Turn left onto W. Meeker Street and continue for 0.6 mile. Then turn left onto Russell Road and drive 0.2 mile to parking and the trailhead.

Other Trail Access Points: The following trailheads all have parking: Cecil Moses Memorial Park (Tukwila/Seattle line) at 27th Avenue S. off of SR 99 (West Marginal Way S.); Bicentennial Park (Tukwila) off of Strander Boulevard; Briscoe Park (Kent) off of S. 190th Street; Three Friends Fishing Hole Park (Kent) off of S. 200th Street; Van Doren's Landing Park (Kent) off of Russell Road; and Foster Park (Kent), off S. 259th Street.

Transit: King County Metro routes 150 and 154 stop near Fort Dent Park; routes 158, 159, 166, and 183 stop near Hogan Park

The Green River Trail follows alongside its namesake for nearly 20 miles from the Duwamish River near Seattle to farms and forest south of Kent. While the Green River Valley is heavily developed, the trail south of Tukwila is ringed with greenbelts, parks, historic sites, and remnant farms offering glimpses of the past, when this area was Seattle's bread-basket. This stretch of trail is one of the most delightful long-distance paved trails within the Seattle metropolitan area. (See Trail 38 for map.)

GET MOVING

Like the nearby Interurban Trail (Trail 38), the Green River Trail is popular with bicyclists. But unlike the Interurban, the Green River Trail offers much better running and walking opportunities, largely due to its more abundant natural settings and adjacent parks. For walkers and runners the trail is best experienced from Kent's Hogan Park. The description here is an overview of the trail from north to south.

The trail starts at W. Marginal Place S. just west of S. 102nd Street in Tukwila near the Seattle city limits. At 0.5 mile it passes through Cecil Moses Memorial Park (restrooms, parking) and then crosses the Duwamish River. The way then skirts a Boeing complex before crossing the river once again. The trail then travels along the river, passing apartments, offices, and neighborhoods before paralleling SR 599.

At 2.2 miles it ducks under the historic Allentown bridge, then once again winds through office parks and light-industrial complexes. It cruises under I-5, coming to Interurban Avenue S. at 3.4 miles. It then utilizes a wide sidewalk before resuming trail again, and at 4.5 miles it crosses the Duwamish River and enters Fort Dent Park (restrooms, parking). From here on, the waterway you will be following alongside is the Green River (see sidebar "A River Once Ran Through Here").

The trail continues through manicured lawns in Fort Dent Park before crossing the river and reaching an intersection with the Interurban Trail at 5.6 miles. It then ducks under Interurban Avenue S. and I-405. At 6.4 miles it reaches Bicentennial Park (restrooms, parking) before passing under Strander Boulevard.

The trail then skirts retail outlets and businesses as well as a large wetland. It darts under busy S. 180th Street before crossing over the river. A spur path leads left along the river to SR 181. The Green River Trail continues its snaking course along river bends. At 9.2 miles it reaches a wide bend at Briscoe Park, where there are also some short trails.

Continuing south, the trail passes more warehouses and distribution centers as well as patches of surviving farmland. It ducks safely beneath S. 200th Street, coming to Three Friends Fishing Hole Park (parking, restrooms) at 10.1 miles. After S. 212th Street, the trail is at its best, winding through numerous parks, preserves, and scenic spots where Mount Rainier is usually seen hovering in the distance.

The trail utilizes the lightly trafficked Russell Road for short stretches here. At 11.7 miles the trail passes through Van Doren's Landing Park (parking, restrooms). To the trail's east is the sprawling Green River Natural Resources Area with its miles of soft-surfaced trails. Soon afterward the trail intersects the Puget Power Trail—a paved path leading east for 1.1 miles to SR 181 (West Valley Highway) that will eventually extend to the Interurban Trail. It also passes a footbridge across the river to Frager Road S., which is closed to traffic for most of its way, allowing for loop walks and runs.

After ducking beneath Veterans Drive at 12.6 miles, the trail once again resumes as a path and heads through the towering cottonwoods of Russell Woods Park. It then passes

Remnant rural patch along the Green River Trail

by the restored 1885-built Neely-Soames Historic Homestead, one of the oldest homes in Kent.

At 13.6 miles come to Hogan Park (parking, restrooms).
The trail then skirts the Riverbend Golf Complex, where fencing should spare you from an errant golf ball. At 14.5 miles
come to a junction. The trail right crosses the Green River to
closed-to-cars Frager Road, where you can walk downriver for
a loop.

The Green River Trail continues left, ducking under W.
Meeker Street and SR 516. It then utilizes a tiny stretch of road
before cruising under 68th Avenue S. and traversing Riverview

Park, where a spur crosses the river to 68th Avenue S. Next, the trail travels under SR 167, reaching the Interurban Trail at Foster Park at 17.1 miles.

From here you can carefully walk S. 259th Street to 79th Avenue S. to S. 266th Street to pick up a noncontiguous section of the trail at 18.1 miles. Then on paved trail once more, the way heads under 83rd Avenue S. and skirts residences before ending at 19.6 miles on 94th Place S. (no parking) in a forested area at a big river bend. This is a quiet section of trail with good views south across farmland to Mount Rainier. This is also the end of the trail—for now. King County Parks has plans to extend the trail all the way to Flaming Geyser State Park east of Auburn.

GO FARTHER

Definitely check out the 1.4 miles of trails in the 304-acre Green River Natural Resources Area (parking on Russell Road; check website for hours). In this reclaimed wetland, there are three viewing towers you can hike to from where birding and Rainier viewing are excellent.

40 Soos Creek Trail

DISTANCE:	5.7 miles one-way
ELEVATION GAIN:	550 feet
HIGH POINT:	375 feet
DIFFICULTY:	Easy
FITNESS:	Walkers, runners
FAMILY-FRIENDLY:	Yes, and paved trail is jogger-stroller and wheelchair friendly
DOG-FRIENDLY:	On leash
AMENITIES:	Restrooms, benches
CONTACT/MAP:	King County Parks
GPS:	N47 21.834 W122 08.621

GETTING THERE

Driving to South Trailhead: From Seattle, follow I-5 south to I-405 to SR 167 (Valley Freeway). Drive south on SR 167 for 5 miles, then take the 84th Avenue/Central Avenue exit. Turn left onto Central Avenue N. and drive 1.1 miles. Then turn left onto SR 516 (E. Smith Street eventually becoming SE Kent-Kangley Road) and drive 5 miles. Just past Lake Meridian Park turn left onto 152nd Way SE. Follow this road, which becomes 148th Avenue SE, 0.3 mile to the trailhead and parking on your right.

From Tacoma, follow I-5 north to SR 18. Drive east on SR 18, then exit onto SR 516 (SE 272nd Street). Turn left and drive 0.9 mile. Then turn right onto 152nd Way SE and follow the preceding directions.

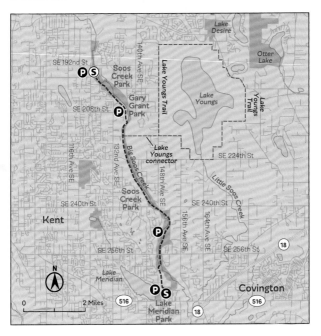

Three generations of hikers take to the Soos Creek Trail.

Driving to Gary Grant Park: From Seattle or Tacoma, follow SR 167 (Valley Freeway) to the S. 212th Street exit. Head west on S. 212th Street, which bends and becomes SE 208th Street, for 3.1 miles to the trailhead and parking on your right.

Other Trail Access Points: Additional trailheads are located off of 148th Avenue SE and 124th Avenue SE.

Transit: King County Metro routes 158, 159, and 168 stop near South Trailhead

Go for an invigorating run or peaceful stroll on all or part of this wonderful paved trail that traverses an emerald ribbon along the eastern edge of Washington's sixth- and eighth-largest cities. Follow alongside Big Soos Creek, passing through meadows, wetlands, handsome groves of conifers, and by small horse farms. Wildlife is abundant along this natural corridor.

GET MOVING

A popular trail, Soos Creek extends south to north for 5.7 miles. There's plenty of room, however, as most walkers just take short strolls to and from the trailheads, leaving quiet stretches of trail. A soft-surface path favored by horseback riders parallels the southern half of the trail. Most of the way is through semirural countryside, a remnant of a South King County long since passed.

From the southern trailhead, the route skirts a few homes and then makes a steep descent (remember for the return). It then crosses the creek and traverses an attractive patch of forest. At 0.7 mile the way crosses (use caution) busy SE 256th Street and reenters forest. At 1.3 miles a paved spur heads left to the 148th Avenue SE Trailhead (parking, restrooms).

The path continues through forest and crosses (use signal) SE 244th Street before descending to make another bridged crossing of Big Soos Creek. At 1.9 miles the trail crosses 148th Avenue SE. Now in attractive forest, it climbs once more and then descends before breaking out into open meadow near a powerline corridor. This stretch is rife with sprawling wetlands.

At 3.2 miles the trail reaches SE 224th Street. Turn right and walk this quiet road for a couple hundred feet, crossing over the creek, then pick up the trail once again. It continues along through wetlands that may cause some flooding during periods of heavy rain. At 3.8 miles come to SE 216th Street. Here you can walk or run right 0.7 mile on quiet road and trail to the Lake Youngs Trail (Trail 42). The Soos Creek Trail continues north, soon making another bridged crossing of the creek before reaching the popular Gary Grant Park Trailhead (restrooms, picnic tables, and parking) at 4.4 miles.

Continuing north, the trail, now via an elevated concrete walkway, traverses more wetlands, coming to busy SE Lake Youngs Way (use signal to cross) at 4.7 miles. The trail then skirts homes and wetlands, going up and over a small hill. At 5.2 miles a spur leads left to a neighborhood. The main trail now follows below high-tension powerlines, coming to the northern trailhead at 124th Avenue SE (parking, restrooms) at 5.7 miles.

King County Parks is planning to eventually extend the trail even farther north to connect it with the Cedar River Trail in Renton.

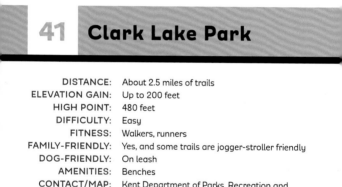

41 Clark Lake Park

DISTANCE:	About 2.5 miles of trails
ELEVATION GAIN:	Up to 200 feet
HIGH POINT:	480 feet
DIFFICULTY:	Easy
FITNESS:	Walkers, runners
FAMILY-FRIENDLY:	Yes, and some trails are jogger-stroller friendly
DOG-FRIENDLY:	On leash
AMENITIES:	Benches
CONTACT/MAP:	Kent Department of Parks, Recreation and Community Services
GPS:	N47 23.196 W122 10.438
BEFORE YOU GO:	Main parking area is small with no parking on SE 240th Street; alternative parking can be found at the trailhead on 120th Avenue SE

GETTING THERE

Driving: From Seattle, follow I-5 south to I-405 to SR 167 (Valley Freeway). Drive south on SR 167 for 5 miles, then take the 84th Avenue/Central Avenue exit. Turn left onto Central

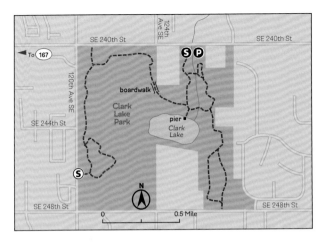

Avenue N. and drive 0.8 mile. Then turn left onto E. James Street (which becomes SE 240th Street) and drive 2.7 miles to the trailhead and parking on your right.

From Tacoma, follow I-5 north to SR 18 to SR 167 (Valley Freeway). Drive 5.5 miles north on SR 167, then take the SR 516/Willis Street exit. Head right on Willis Street for 0.6 mile. Turn left onto Central Avenue S. and proceed for 0.6 mile. Then turn right onto E. James Street and follow the preceding directions.

Transit: King County Metro Route 158 (very limited service) and DART 916

Hit the trail in this 130-acre park and be prepared for plenty of surprises. Surprise number one: a lovely, undeveloped little lake. Number two: delightful views of Mount Rainier and other Cascade peaks from the park's rolling, open terrain. Number three: adjacent farmland, a remnant of when Kent wasn't covered with housing developments and warehouses. And number four: the ridiculously small parking lot for such a popular park. Get here early on sunny days.

Clark Lake's fishing pier

GET MOVING

Managed as a natural area, Clark Lake Park lacks manicured lawns, playfields, and picnic tables. Unfortunately, the park also lacks restrooms and adequate parking. Its trails, how-ever, are designed well and are aesthetically pleasing—they are occasionally lined with split-rail fencing and graced with boardwalks. There are some environmentally themed public art installations in the park too.

From the main wide trail (an old road) head south. You can walk a quick 0.2 mile straight to the lake. Here a fishing pier provides the best access (swimming prohibited) and viewing of the small 7-acre lake. Just before you reach the lake, a pair of short loop trails and one longer lollypop loop trail diverge. If you head to the left you'll soon come to a junction. The trail left swings through pleasant woods and crosses a creek, returning to the main trail near the park entrance in 0.25 mile.

The trail right crosses a creek on a boardwalk, climbs some steps, and then at 0.1 mile splits. Go either way on this

0.6-mile loop. You'll climb about 70 feet or so through old pasture. There are some pastoral views of a small farm to the west and the lake to the north.

The lollypop loop trail leaves west from the pier, soon crossing a wetland teeming with spirea on a long boardwalk. An old farm lies to the right. The trail then makes a climb through a forested grove before descending and entering an old orchard. A spur heads right to SE 240th Street. The main trail continues left, soon bending south and heading up rolling slopes of young trees and former pasture. At 0.6 mile it reaches a junction where the loop begins. If you go left, you'll drop a bit and then start climbing again, swinging back in a third of a mile to the junction. Along the way you'll pass the 120th Avenue SE Trailhead, a patch of big trees, and some great views of Mount Rainier and the rolling terrain of Clark Lake Park.

42 Lake Youngs Trail

DISTANCE:	9.5-mile loop
ELEVATION GAIN:	950 feet
HIGH POINT:	625 feet
DIFFICULTY:	Easy
FITNESS:	Walkers, runners
FAMILY-FRIENDLY:	Yes; most of the trail is suitable for jogger-strollers
DOG-FRIENDLY:	On leash
AMENITIES:	Restrooms, benches
CONTACT/MAP:	King County Parks
GPS:	N47 26.326 W122 07.194
BEFORE YOU GO:	Be aware that the trail is popular with mountain bikers and equestrians

GETTING THERE

Driving: From Seattle, follow I-5 south (from Tacoma, follow I-5 north) to I-405 and take exit 4. Turn right onto SR 169

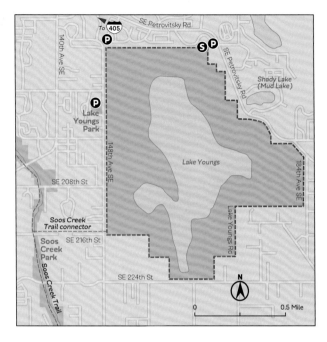

and drive 2.5 miles. Then turn right onto 140th Way SE (which becomes 140th Avenue SE) and follow for 2 miles. Next turn left onto SE Petrovitsky Road and proceed for 1.9 miles. Then turn right onto SE 184th Street (which soon becomes SE Old Petrovitsky Road) and continue 0.2 mile to trailhead and parking.

You won't see much of Lake Youngs on this long loop trail. You will, however, get a good workout in if you run or hike the entire trail circumnavigating the gated reservoir. While suburbia has encroached upon the area, much of the trail still abuts forest and wetlands. And more than likely, you'll be greeted by a few *deer* friends along the way.

Big trees line the way along Lake Youngs Trail.

GET MOVING

The Lake Youngs Trail is actually a graveled maintenance perimeter road for the 790-acre Lake Youngs Reservoir. The reservoir was created in the 1920s by the Seattle Water Department (now Seattle Public Utilities) by damming and enlarging Swan Lake (since renamed after the department superintendent responsible for the reservoir). Water from the Cedar River is piped into the lake, where it is held to avert shortages during low-flow periods.

There is no public access to the lake. A thick forested buffer and perimeter gate surround the reservoir. The trail travels along the gate, crossing the outtake and intake pipelines. Nearly the entire view inward toward the lake will be of mature second-growth forest. You might catch a tiny glimpse or two of the lake (although it's best viewed by taking a plane in or out of Sea-Tac Airport!).

The views outward include forest, wetlands, horse farms, and some rural residences as well as a stretch of high-density suburbia. From the trailhead follow a 0.1-mile trail leading to the perimeter trail. From here either go left or right for a 9.3-mile loop. The loop is hilly in places but never steep. There are long gentle stretches too. Almost the entire trail is wide gravel road that is good for pushing a jogger-stroller. But there is a 2-mile stretch (beginning about 1.2 miles left from the junction) of singletrack, which is rocky at times and close to busy Petrovitsky Road. If you are looking to do an out and back with a stroller, go right from the junction.

The most attractive part of the trail is along the southern perimeter, where it travels for stretches through forest and away from roads. The trail makes sharp 90-degree turns along the periphery, and mileage markers are posted along the way. The western section of the trail, which includes some good hills, runs parallel with 148th Avenue SE. If you want to just hike or run this stretch of trail, there are several places you can park here—at the small Lake Youngs Park and at a lot on 148th Avenue SE where it bends to become SE 183rd Street.

GO FARTHER

Where the trail bends north upon reaching 148th Avenue SE, it is possible to continue west 0.7 mile on quiet SE 216th Street (with a small trail connecting two noncontiguous sections of this road) to connect with the Soos Creek Trail (Trail 40). Ultrarunners take note!

43 Gene Coulon Memorial Beach Park

DISTANCE:	1.5 miles of trails
ELEVATION GAIN:	Minimal
HIGH POINT:	30 feet
DIFFICULTY:	Easy
FITNESS:	Walkers, runners
FAMILY-FRIENDLY:	Yes
DOG-FRIENDLY:	Dogs prohibited
AMENITIES:	Restrooms, picnic shelters, playground, interpretive signs, swimming beach, summer concessionaire
CONTACT/MAP:	City of Renton Parks Commission
GPS:	N47 30.399 W122 12.138
BEFORE YOU GO:	Park is open from 8:00 AM to dusk

GETTING THERE

Driving: From Seattle, follow I-5 south to I-405 and take exit 5. Turn left onto NE Park Drive and proceed for 0.3 mile. Then turn right onto Lake Washington Boulevard N. and continue for 0.2 mile to the park and plenty of parking.

Transit: King County Metro routes RapidRide F, 167, 240, and 342 all stop near the NE Park Drive/Lake Washington Boulevard intersection

One of the finest parks on Lake Washington, the Gene Coulon Memorial Beach Park contains one of the prettiest lakeshore walks in the Seattle metropolitan area. Walk a paved path through impeccably landscaped grounds, passing an array of impressive trees both native and exotic. Pass too historic remnants of a time when the lake boomed with logs.

GET MOVING

As the large parking lots attest, Gene Coulon Park is a popular place, especially on a warm summer day. But come here

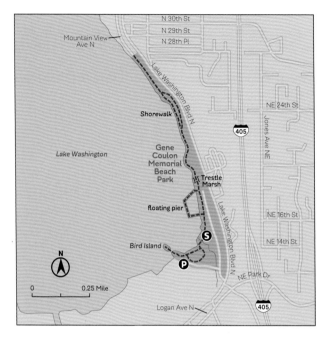

early in the morning or in the dead of winter and share this gorgeous lakefront park with just a handful of kindred souls. The park is small—57 acres—but it is spread out along a mile of lakeshore. And there is so much to see here. Its 1.5 miles of trails are meant to be strolled, not sprinted.

Start by heading over to tiny Bird Island, just past the play area. Then pass the swimming area, boat launch, pavilions, and concessions and come to the start of the shore trail. This entire area once staged docks where coal was dumped into barges and timber was dumped into a log boom. In the 1960s civic leaders envisioned the area transformed from its industrial past into a recreational future. The park was named in honor of longtime Renton Parks Director Gene Coulon.

Professionally landscaped, the park contains quite an array of trees. There are sequoias, bald cypresses, tulip poplars, live oaks, and so many other intriguing trees from across the country and beyond. Download the park's botanical brochure to take with you for tree identification.

Walk across lawns and past attractive tree groves on rolling shoreline. Cross a bridge at the Trestle Marsh, a natural area that was once the log dump. Stroll along the Shorewalk, a trestle across a small cove. Look for a myriad of bird life and some small mammals as well. And look out across the lake to the Olympics and back over your shoulder to Mount Rainier. Sunsets are simply sublime here. A long log boom remains in

Hikers on the park's Shorewalk

place—now to keep boats at a safe distance. The shore trail is less than a mile, ending at the park's north gate on Mountain View Avenue N.

On your return extend your walk by sauntering out on the 900-foot floating pier. It's a squared pier, giving you an opportunity to walk on water. Kids will love it. You will too.

44   Cedar River Trail

DISTANCE:	17.3 miles one-way
ELEVATION GAIN:	Up to 550 feet
HIGH POINT:	550 feet
DIFFICULTY:	Easy
FITNESS:	Walkers, runners
FAMILY-FRIENDLY:	Yes
DOG-FRIENDLY:	Yes
AMENITIES:	Restrooms, picnic shelters, playground
CONTACT/MAP:	King County Parks
GPS:	N47 29.980 W122 12.895
BEFORE YOU GO:	Cedar River Park (Nishiwaki Lane) closes at dusk

GETTING THERE

Driving: From Seattle, follow I-5 south to exit 157. Continue east on SR 900 (Martin Luther King Jr. Way S., which becomes SW Sunset Boulevard) for 3.5 miles. Turn left onto Rainier Avenue S. and proceed for 0.4 mile. Then turn right onto Airport Way (which becomes Logan Avenue N.) and continue for 0.9 mile. Next, turn left onto N. 6th Street (which becomes Nishiwaki Lane) and drive 0.4 mile to parking and the trailhead.

From Tacoma, follow SR 167 north (passing the I-405 junction) to Rainier Avenue S. Then follow the preceding directions from Rainier Avenue.

Other Trail Access Points (all have parking): Cedar River Park off of Houser Way N., Riverview Park (off of SR 169), Ron Regis Park (off of SR 169), and the parking area off of SR 169 just north of the SR 18 overpass.

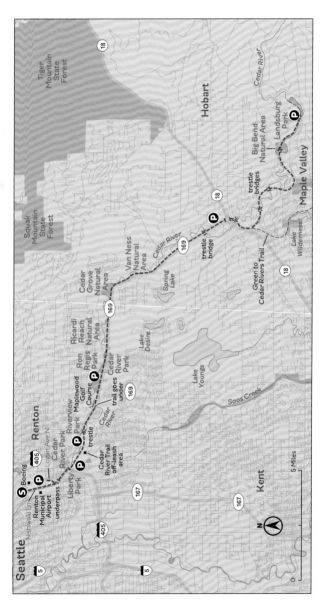

Transit: King County Metro routes 167 and 240 access the trail at Liberty Park; routes 143 and 907 access the trail at various stops along SR 169 (Maple Valley Highway)

Walk or run from Lake Washington all the way to Landsburg at the boundary of Seattle's Cedar River Watershed. While the majority of this mostly paved trail parallels the busy Maple Valley Highway and is more appealing to bicyclists than pedestrians, the western 3 miles or so within the Renton city limits are a pure delight to walk or run. Here you'll find an attractive brick riverside path that feels like it is straight out of Europe. And just beyond, the path traverses an emerald hollow that is pure Northwest wild.

GET MOVING

The Cedar River Trail begins as a paved path in a beautifully landscaped park along the Cedar River wedged between the Renton Airport and Boeing's Renton plant. From the river's outlet in Lake Washington, start your walk or run upstream. Catch a lake view first before heading out.

The path begins as pedestrian-only, paralleling Nishiwaki Lane (named for Renton's Japanese Sister City). At 0.5 mile bikes are now allowed to use the trail as it passes by Renton Memorial Stadium. The path then ducks under Logan Avenue N., passes the Senior Activity Center, and splits in two. Bikes are relegated to the left (upper) path while pedestrians are sent to the lower path on a brick walkway right at water's edge (so close that the trail frequently floods) beneath a canopy of shading sycamore trees. It is one of the nicest urban walks in Washington—and one that has a European ambience—perfect for a *passeggiata*.

There is a parallel path across the river for short loops, but the main trail ducks beneath three road bridges (all with staircases leading to them if you want to spice up your workout), coming to Liberty Park at 1.5 miles. Here the Renton Library

Brick-constructed trail through Renton

spans the river. And notice the river is now no longer flowing through a canal (see sidebar "A River Once Ran Through Here"). Continue through the park and cross Houser Way N.

at its crosswalk. Then walk on the Cedar Park access road, passing under I-405. Here pick up the Cedar River Trail once again by heading right on a bridge crossing the river.

The path then turns left, passing a parking area and off-leash dog park. Following a railroad bed—part of the same line that is now the Iron Horse Trail across Snoqualmie Pass—the way enters thick forest at the base of steep slopes cut by small cascades. It is a pretty wild setting—and so close to downtown Renton. At 2.7 miles is a spur leading left to a picnic shelter and bridge across the river to Riverview Park and parking.

The Cedar River Trail continues east, soon coming to a trestle spanning the river. This is a good point to turn around if you're looking for a short run or walk. Beyond, the route parallels busy SR 169 for quite some distance. While the river is almost always in view—and quite scenic—the highway noise can at times be unsettling.

The trail crosses the river again and swings under SR 169 to parallel it on its westbound side. The trail then reaches Ron Regis Park (parking, restrooms) at 4.6 miles. Next it darts under busy 154th Place SE and travels beside towering cottonwoods and other trees gracing a second Cedar River Park, Ricardi Reach Natural Area, and Cedar Grove Natural Area. The river churns and ripples as you slowly ascend alongside it.

At 8.2 miles check out the short split-rail-lined path leading left to an overlook where bald eagles are frequently observed. This entire area was once a homestead and is now part of Seattle Public Utilities' (who owns and manages the upper Cedar River Watershed for Seattle's water supply) Van Ness Natural Area.

The Cedar River Trail continues along SR 169, crossing busy Cedar Grove Road SE (use signal) and then the river on a trestle at 10.9 miles. It passes a parking area at 11.6 miles before traveling beneath SR 18 and SE 216th Way. Now pulling away from roads, the trail makes a trestle crossing of the river before coming to a junction and pavement end at 12.4 miles. The way right is the Green to Cedar Rivers Trail, which travels to Maple Valley.

The Cedar River Trail, now soft-surfaced, travels left, traversing forest and rural countryside. It crosses the river three more times on century-old trestles and passes through the Big Bend Natural Area before terminating at 17.3 miles at Landsburg Park.

45 Spring Lake/ Lake Desire and McGarvey Parks

DISTANCE:	More than 11 miles of trails
ELEVATION GAIN:	Up to 1000 feet
HIGH POINT:	896 feet
DIFFICULTY:	Easy to moderate
FITNESS:	Hikers, runners
FAMILY-FRIENDLY:	Yes
DOG-FRIENDLY:	On leash
AMENITIES:	Restrooms
CONTACT/MAP:	King County Parks
GPS:	N47 26.220 W122 05.656
BEFORE YOU GO:	Don't block gates at small parking area; Discover Pass required at the adjacent Spring Lake boat launch parking area

GETTING THERE

Driving: From Seattle, follow I-5 south to I-405 and take exit 4. Turn right onto SR 169 and drive 6.3 miles. Then turn right onto 196th Avenue SE and follow for 1.7 miles. Next turn right onto SE 183rd Street and after a few hundred feet immediately turn right onto East Spring Lake Drive SE. Follow for 1 mile to its end and the trailhead.

There are plenty of trails to explore in this more-than-1000-acre greenbelt on the edge of Renton. And despite the size of this recreation and conservation area and its proximity to population centers, its trails are not overrun. Explore bogs, mature second-growth forest, lakeshore, and a little summit (the highest point in this book) that sports a wide array of flora and a view of Mount Rainier.

GET MOVING

Be sure to download a map of the area before setting off, as signage is sparse in these parks. In general the trails within Spring Lake/Lake Desire Park are more popular with hikers and runners, and the ones in adjacent McGarvey Park Open

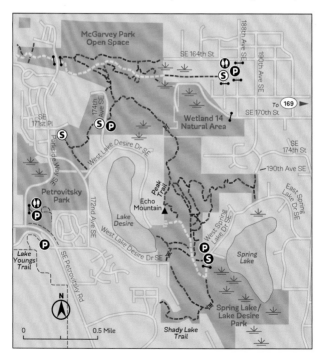

Space see more mountain-bike use. All the trails except the Peak Trail are open to bikes and horses. The trails within Spring Lake/Lake Desire tend to be better built (thanks to groups like the Washington Trails Association), and they traverse more interesting and attractive terrain. Nevertheless, McGarvey Park has a few desirable trails too—and if you are looking for an all-day hike or a long, challenging run, you'll want to take to most of that park's trails.

The most popular destination within these parks is Echo (Cedar) Mountain. To reach this little 896-foot peak, follow the main trail (gated water tower service road) for 0.5 mile to the Peak Trail (signed). Then head about 0.2 mile up to the ledgy and forested summit. The forest is reclaiming much of this old bald, encroaching on the views. But Rainier still can be seen, and you catch a few glimpses of the Issaquah Alps and of Lake Desire below. The real attraction of this peak is its unique flora and spring wildflowers, including chocolate lilies. Keep your travels on rock and ledge to protect the fragile vegetation.

The Peak Trail continues 0.2 mile down off of the north side of the mountain, reaching a junction. From here you can head right 0.7 mile back to the trailhead or connect to other trails. The trails heading east are worth checking out. They travel around and over an 800-plus-foot knob. It lacks views but its forest is particularly attractive, approaching old-growth status. There's a 0.5-mile trail that leads off of that peak to spurs terminating on 190th Avenue SE and East Spring Lake Drive SE (no parking), from where you can walk the road right 0.5 mile or so back to the trailhead.

From the Peak Trail's northern junction you can also head left on a well-built and generally peaceful trail. It passes old cuts and crosses a creek flowing between the Wetland 14 Natural Area and Lake Desire. At 1 mile this trail comes to a junction. The way left reaches 174th Avenue SE (parking) in 0.1 mile and then continues up and over a small rise, coming

Hiker in mature cedar grove

to another junction in 0.4 mile. From here it's 0.16 mile right to a neighborhood or 0.17 mile left to West Lake Desire Drive SE.

The way right from the aforementioned junction just before 174th Avenue SE follows an old skid road, reaching a power-line swath in 0.25 mile. Here a gated service road and parallel trails head left and right beneath and along the swath. It's not that appealing, but if you're a runner, you may appreciate the options to add extra miles. If you follow the service-road trail right for 0.8 mile, it will take you to Maple Valley Heights Park, where there is parking and a restroom.

Back at the main trailhead, another hiking option is a 1.2-mile loop that branches off of the water tower service road. This path skirts a large bog containing Labrador tea and other plants uncommon to this region. Near a bridged crossing of a small creek there is a small 0.15-mile spur trail leading west to a small section of house-free shoreline along Lake Desire. The trail also connects to the brand new (2017 built) 0.5 mile Shady Lake Trail leading to 179th Place SE.

Seattle skyline across Lake Union from Gas Works Park (Trail 18)

ACKNOWLEDGMENTS

RESEARCHING AND WRITING *URBAN TRAILS: SEATTLE* was fun, gratifying, and a lot of hard work. I couldn't have finished this project without the help and support of the following people. A huge thank-you to all the great people at Mountaineers Books, especially publisher Helen Cherullo, editor-in-chief Kate Rogers, and project manager Melissa Kiepke.

A big thank-you to my copyeditor, Rebecca Jaynes, for her attention to detail and thoughtful suggestions, helping to make this book a finer volume. I also want to thank my wife, Heather, and son, Giovanni, for accompanying me on many of the trails in this book. A big thanks too to Richard and Judith Romano, Suzanne Gerber, Nakean and Craiggan Wickloff, Susan Elderkin, Melissa Ozbek, Krista Hudson, Virginia Scott, and Bob Wismer for providing me with excellent trail company. Big thanks to Matt Fraser for taking me sailing to Blake Island. And thanks so much to Julie Grunwald with the Vashon-Maury Island Land Trust and David Kimmett with King County Parks for their invaluable help. And I thank God for watching over me and keeping me safe and healthy while I hiked and ran all over Seattle and its environs!

Steps in Frink Park (Trail 12)

RESOURCES

CONTACTS AND MAPS

Argosy Cruises
Blake Island
www.argosycruises.com/argosy-cruises/tillicum-excursion

City of Burien
Seahurst Park
http://burienwa.gov/facilities/Facility/Details/19

City of Des Moines
Des Moines Creek Trail
www.desmoineswa.gov/Facilities/Facility/Details/4

City of Kent
Clark Lake Park
www.kentwa.gov/Home/Components/FacilityDirectory
/FacilityDirectory/270/318?selcat=73

Green River Natural Resources Area
www.kentwa.gov/government/public-works/grnra

City of Renton
Gene Coulon Memorial Beach Park
http://rentonwa.gov/living/default.aspx?id=74

City of SeaTac
North SeaTac Park
www.ci.seatac.wa.us/index.aspx?page=144

City of Seattle
Alki Trail
www.seattle.gov/transportation/alkitrail.htm

Camp Long
www.seattle.gov/parks/find/centers/camp-long

Duwamish Trail
www.kingcounty.gov/services/gis/Maps/vmc/Recreation.aspx

Seattle Parks and Recreation Hiking Trails Maps
www.seattle.gov/parks/find/hiking-and-trails

Seattle Parks Directory
www.seattle.gov/parks/find/parks

City of Shoreline
Boeing Creek Park
http://cosweb.ci.shoreline.wa.us/uploads/attachments
/par/webparks/boeingcreektrailmap.pdf

Hamlin Park
http://cascadeoc.org/wp-content/uploads/2016/05
/perm-Hamlin.pdf

Duwamish Longhouse and Cultural Center
www.duwamishtribe.org

King County Metro Transit
http://kingcounty.gov/depts/transportation/metro.aspx

King County Parks
Dockton Forest and Maury Island Natural Area
www.kingcounty.gov/services/parks-recreation/parks/parks
-and-natural-lands/natural-lands/maury-island-natural.aspx

King County Parks Directory
www.kingcounty.gov/services/parks-recreation/parks/trails
/regional-trails/popular-trails

Lake Youngs Trail
www.kingcounty.gov/services/gis/Maps/vmc/Recreation.aspx

Maury Island Marine Park
www.kingcounty.gov/services/parks-recreation/parks
/parks-and-natural-lands/natural-lands/maury-island
-marine-park.aspx

Shinglemill Creek Preserve
http://your.kingcounty.gov/ftp/gis/Web/VMC/recreation
/BCT_Shinglemill_brochure.pdf

Spring Lake/Lake Desire and McGarvey Parks
http://your.kingcounty.gov/ftp/gis/Web/VMC/recreation
/BCT_SpringLkMcGarvey_brochure.pdf

Port of Seattle
Centennial Park (Elliott Bay Trail)
www.portseattle.org/Parks-Public-Access/Parks/Pages
/Centennial-Park.aspx

Jack Block Park (Alki Trail)
www.portseattle.org/Parks-Public-Access/Parks/Pages
/Jack-Block-Park.aspx

Terminal 107 Park (Duwamish Trail)
www.portseattle.org/Parks-Public-Access/Parks/Pages
/Terminal-107-Park.aspx

Seattle Department of Transportation
Chief Sealth Trail
www.seattle.gov/transportation/chiefsealthtrail.htm

University of Washington Botanic Gardens
Union Bay Natural Area
https://botanicgardens.uw.edu/center-for-urban
-horticulture/visit/union-bay-natural-area

Washington Park Arboretum
https://botanicgardens.uw.edu/washington-park-arboretum

Vashon-Maury Island Land Trust
Fisher Pond
http://vashonlandtrust.org/portfolio-item/fisher-pond

Judd Creek
http://vashonlandtrust.org/portfolio-item/judd-creek2

Vashon Park District
Burton Acres Park
https://vashonparks.org/burton-acres

Point Robinson Park
https://vashonparks.org/point-robinson

Washington State Parks
Blake Island Marine State Park
http://parks.state.wa.us/476/Blake-Island

Saltwater State Park
http://parks.state.wa.us/578/Saltwater

TRAIL AND CONSERVATION ORGANIZATIONS

Arboretum Foundation
www.arboretumfoundation.org

Forterra
http://forterra.org

Friends of the Burke-Gilman Trail
www.burkegilmantrail.org

Friends of Deadhorse Canyon
www.facebook.com/FriendsOfDeadhorseCanyon

Friends of Discovery Park
www.seattlediscoverypark.org

Friends of Frink Park
www.frinkpark.org

Friends of Schmitz Park
www.facebook.com/friendsofschmitzpark

Friends of Seward Park
www.sewardpark.org/friends.html

Friends of Yesler Swamp
http://yeslerswamp.org

Kubota Garden Foundation
www.kubotagarden.org

The Mountaineers
www.mountaineers.org

Mountains to Sound Greenway
http://mtsgreenway.org

The Nature Conservancy
www.nature.org

Seattle Parks Foundation
www.seattleparksfoundation.org

Seward Park Audubon Center
http://sewardpark.audubon.org

Sustainability Ambassadors
www.sustainabilityambassadors.org

Vashon-Maury Island Land Trust
www.vashonlandtrust.org

Washington State Parks Foundation
http://wspf.org

Washington Trails Association
www.wta.org

Washington Wildlife and Recreation Coalition
www.wildliferecreation.org

West Duwamish Greenbelt Trails
https://wdgtrails.wordpress.com

RUNNING AND HIKING CLUBS AND ORGANIZED RUNS, HIKES, AND WALKS IN AND AROUND SEATTLE

Christmas Rush Fun Run and Walk

5K and 10K run sponsored by Kent Parks, Recreation and Community Services, held on the Green River Trail.
www.kentwa.gov/residents/parks-recreation-and-community
-services/events/christmas-rush-fun-run-and-walk

Furry 5K Run

Dog-friendly run benefitting the Seattle Animal Shelter, held at Seward Park.
www.furry5k.com

Green River Marathon

26.2-mile run on the Green River Trail from Kent to Alki Beach.
www.greenrivermarathon.com

Hike It Baby

National organization with chapters in Seattle and South King County, focusing on group hikes with infants and toddlers.
https://hikeitbaby.com

Interurban Runners Club

South King County running club that organizes group runs and sponsors a summer race series on the Green River Trail.
www.interurbanrunners.net

Kent Cornucopia Days 5K

5K run sponsored by Kent Parks, Recreation and Community Services, held on the Green River Trail.
www.kentwa.gov/residents/parks-recreation-and
-community-services/events/kent-cornucopia-days-5k

Magnuson Series
Monthly races of varying distances, held at Magnuson Park.
www.magnusonseries.org

The Mountaineers
Seattle-based outdoor club involved with local conservation
issues as well as coordinating group outdoor activities.
www.mountaineers.org

Northwest Trail Runs
Well-organized series of trail runs that includes races
at Woodland Park, Ravenna Park, Seward Park, and
Carkeek Park.
http://nwtrailruns.com/events

Outdoor Afro Seattle
A community that reconnects African Americans with
naturcl spaces and one another through a wide array of
recreational activities, including hiking.
www.meetup.com/Outdoor-Afro-Seattle

Resolution Run
5K New Year's Day run at Magnuson Park.
http://promotionevents.com/resorun/default.htm

Seattle Frontrunners
LGBTQ running and walking club (open to all) that sponsors
weekly runs at Green Lake and annual Pride Run and Walk
at Seward Park.
www.seattlefrontrunners.org

Seattle Green Lake Running Group
The name says it all—a large social group that meets
at Seattle's most popular running destination.
www.meetup.com/Seattle-Greenlake-Running-Group

**Seattle Parks and Recreation Sound Steps
Walking Program**
Organized walks and programs for folks fifty and older.
www.seattle.gov/parks/find/sounds-steps-(50)

Seattle Running Club
Large club dedicated to trail running; SRC stages weekly
group runs, several annual races, and volunteer trail-work
parties.
https://seattlerunningclub.org

Seven Hills Running Shop
Specialty running store near Discovery Park that supports
the local trail-running community through events and
donations to WTA.
http://sevenhillsrunningshop.com

Shore Run
10K run along the Lake Washington Trail and through Leschi
Park benefitting Fred Hutchinson Cancer Research Center.
http://shorerun.com

Super Jock 'n Jill
Seattle's oldest running specialty store sponsors evening
runs and programs at Green Lake.
https://superjocknjill.com

Discovery Park's North Beach Trail (Trail 16)

INDEX

Author Craig Romano and family

ABOUT THE AUTHOR

Craig Romano grew up in rural New Hampshire, where he fell in love with the natural world. He moved to Washington in 1989 and has since hiked more than 20,000 miles in the Evergreen State. An avid runner as well, Craig has run more than twenty-five marathons and ultra runs, including the Boston Marathon and the White River 50 Mile Endurance Run. Craig lived in Seattle for years, attended the University of Washington, and ran the city's trails in between work and classes.

Craig is an award-winning author and co-author of nineteen books. His *Columbia Highlands, Exploring Washington's Last Frontier* was recognized in 2010 by Washington Secretary of State Sam Reed and State Librarian Jan Walsh as a "Washington Reads" book for its contribution to Washington's cultural heritage. Craig also writes for numerous publications, tourism websites, and Hikeoftheweek.com.

When not hiking, running, and writing, he can be found napping with his wife, Heather; son, Giovanni; and cat, Giuseppe, at his home in Skagit County. Visit him at http://CraigRomano.com and on Facebook at "Craig Romano Guidebook Author."

recreation · lifestyle · conservation

MOUNTAINEERS BOOKS, including its two imprints, Skipstone and Braided River, is a leading publisher of quality outdoor recreation, sustainability, and conservation titles. As a 501(c)(3) nonprofit, we are committed to supporting the environmental and educational goals of our organization by providing expert information on human-powered adventure, sustainable practices at home and on the trail, and preservation of wilderness.

Our publications are made possible through the generosity of donors, and through sales of more than 800 titles on outdoor recreation, sustainable lifestyle, and conservation. To donate, purchase books, or learn more, visit us online:

MOUNTAINEERS BOOKS
1001 SW Klickitat Way, Suite 201 • Seattle, WA 98134
800-553-4453 • mbooks@mountaineersbooks.org
www.mountaineersbooks.org

 Leave No Trace strives to educate visitors about the nature of their recreational impacts and offers techniques to prevent and minimize such impacts. Leave No Trace is best understood as an educational and ethical program, not as a set of rules and regulations. For more information, visit www.lnt.org or call 800-332-4100.